McCall's Book
of Wonderful
One-Dish Meals

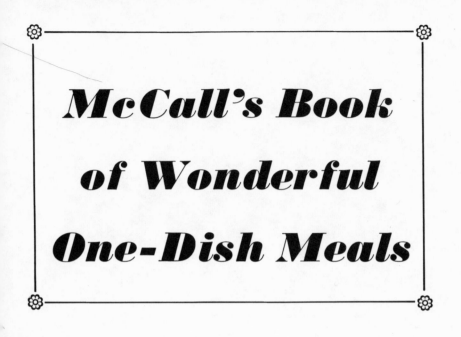

McCall's Book of Wonderful One-Dish Meals

EDITED BY

KAY SULLIVAN

Saturday Review Press
New York

Published simultaneously in Canada by Doubleday Canada
Ltd., Toronto.

Library of Congress Catalog Card Number: 71-182483
ISBN 0-8415-0159-9

Saturday Review Press

PRINTED IN THE UNITED STATES OF AMERICA

Design by Margaret F. Plympton

Contents

❀ ❀ ❀

Foreword

❀ ❀ ❀

We have written—and you are reading—this cookbook in exceptional times. Food-wise, we mean.

It's the space age, and men have gone to the moon and walked over its rocks and dunes, gaining the strength and energy to do so from a remarkable supply of condensed and fortified foods. Some of these scientific foods have already found their way to terrestrial marketplaces and no doubt more will.

It is also the jet age, the era of 747s, charter flights, seven-countries-in-six-days arrangements. While you sit comfortably in your kitchen, enjoying an old-fashioned cinnamon doughnut and a second cup of coffee, hundreds if not thousands of your fellow Americans are flying to foreign countries for pleasure or business. These travelers will acquire a taste for exotic dishes that were probably unknown to their grand-parents, and they will bring home memories of native specialties—Saltimbocca, Kedgeree, Moussaka. And soon kitchens on Pine Street, Maple Street, and lots of other tree-lined thoroughfares across the country will echo to the clatter of such sophisticated equipment as duck presses, terrines, marmites.

Then too it's the day of Women's Lib. With equal opportunity, equal pay, women are less inclined to stay at home to do what has long been tagged "woman's work." That old slogan "Let George do it!" is in vogue again. Thus, our cookbook has a double value because it covers both bases. Easy one-dish meals for the liberated lady to prepare so that she does not have to spend all day in the kitchen. And even easier one-dish meals to aid novice George as he encounters soup bones, roux, and shallots for the first time.

What we are saying is that these are times when food—its style, preparation, and consumption—is changing radically. Most of us expect great variety in our daily menus. We have learned to appreciate international dishes. We have also learned to count on convenience foods to make the vital task of feeding a family less complicated. And because we are used to more leisure time, more travel, more entertainment sources, we don't want to spend long hours shuttling from supermarket to stove to table.

That is why this collection of one-dish meals has been put together. The recipes included offer a broad spectrum of cuisines. They are also easy and economical to prepare since they involve a single main course. And in almost every instance, they are remarkably quick to assemble. We call them "Wonderful One-Dish Meals." Because they are.

Kay Sullivan

Foreword

❀ ❀ ❀

We have written—and you are reading—this cookbook in exceptional times. Food-wise, we mean.

It's the space age, and men have gone to the moon and walked over its rocks and dunes, gaining the strength and energy to do so from a remarkable supply of condensed and fortified foods. Some of these scientific foods have already found their way to terrestrial marketplaces and no doubt more will.

It is also the jet age, the era of 747s, charter flights, seven-countries-in-six-days arrangements. While you sit comfortably in your kitchen, enjoying an old-fashioned cinnamon doughnut and a second cup of coffee, hundreds if not thousands of your fellow Americans are flying to foreign countries for pleasure or business. These travelers will acquire a taste for exotic dishes that were probably unknown to their grandparents, and they will bring home memories of native specialties— Saltimbocca, Kedgeree, Moussaka. And soon kitchens on Pine Street, Maple Street, and lots of other tree-lined thoroughfares across the country will echo to the clatter of such sophisticated equipment as duck presses, terrines, marmites.

Then too it's the day of Women's Lib. With equal opportunity, equal pay, women are less inclined to stay at home to do what has long been tagged "woman's work." That old slogan "Let George do it!" is in vogue again. Thus, our cookbook has a double value because it covers both bases. Easy one-dish meals for the liberated lady to prepare so that she does not have to spend all day in the kitchen. And even easier one-dish meals to aid novice George as he encounters soup bones, roux, and shallots for the first time.

What we are saying is that these are times when food—its style, preparation, and consumption—is changing radically. Most of us expect great variety in our daily menus. We have learned to appreciate international dishes. We have also learned to count on convenience foods to make the vital task of feeding a family less complicated. And because we are used to more leisure time, more travel, more entertainment sources, we don't want to spend long hours shuttling from supermarket to stove to table.

That is why this collection of one-dish meals has been put together. The recipes included offer a broad spectrum of cuisines. They are also easy and economical to prepare since they involve a single main course. And in almost every instance, they are remarkably quick to assemble. We call them "Wonderful One-Dish Meals." Because they are.

Kay Sullivan

McCall's Book
of Wonderful
One-Dish Meals

Introduction

It's Just Simple Arithmetic

❀ ❀ ❀

Let's face it: today's homemaker spends enough time juggling figures to qualify for an accountant's job. Between keeping the family budget balanced and wrestling with food quantities, prices, and weights and measurements, she's a one-woman computer.

Marketing, literally, is a day of reckoning for her. At the meat department she has to figure out quickly such things as how much three and a half pounds of stew meat will cost if one pound is eighty-nine cents. And if sixteen people are coming to the party, will a fourteen-pound turkey be too much or a twelve-pound one too little? Canned goods with conflicting net weights lay traps for her. The fruit and vegetable counters challenge her mental dexterity with oddly marked pounds and pints; the dairy counter threatens her sanity with a choice of egg weights. Should she buy the thirty-ounce-to-the-dozen size or save money on the eighteen-ounce-to-the-dozen ones?

At home in the haven of her kitchen, the numbers game continues. There are oven temperatures and timers to contend with and measuring cups and spoons to match up with recipe directions, most of which are incredibly loaded with fractions. In fact, after trying to halve recipes that begin "Take 3¾ tablespoons of . . ." she may give up and make more than she needs of some dish. Even the blender throws in a body punch. Instead of low, medium, and high, the speeds are numbered from one to twelve. Let her pick the wrong button and she gets meringue on her eyebrows.

In the midst of such mathematical complexities, thank heaven, then, for the one-dish meal. It involves just plain simple arithmetic.

No desperate multiplication of ingredients on the grocery bag.

No surreptitious counting on the fingers to figure out portions.

One visit to the supermarket for the makings.

One session in the kitchen getting it ready.

One trip to the table when it's time to serve dinner.

It's absolutely true that one-dish cookery can revolutionize a home-maker's existence. For starters, it can introduce her to her husband and children again, not to mention letting guests see more of her than that glimpse through the swinging door. (That's the swinging door to the kitchen we're talking about—at any meal the busy cook can give it quite a workout, starting with the soup course and going on right through the Mousse au Chocolat.) The annoying thing is how the door stays open just long enough for her to overhear what's being said about her at the table. Pitying little murmurs between mouthfuls of Lobster Quiche about "poor Lucy—always stuck out in that hot kitchen—but she loves it!"

Well, just wait until poor Lucy discovers the character and scope of one-dish meals. She'll be the first one at the table, able to be the gracious hostess on center stage instead of behind the scenes.

By the way, don't take the term *one-dish meal* too literally. It doesn't necessarily mean you'll be able to put a single casserole, bowl, or platter of food in the center of your table and let it go at that. One-dish meals are substantial, but you will still want to surround most of them with some extras, like a green salad, crusty French bread or sweet rolls, or a side dish of rice or noodles, depending on what your choice of one-dish magic has been. And, of course, there will be many times when you will want to add a dessert to round out the meal, particularly if your family has that all-American malady, the "sweet tooth." The real implication of one-dish cookery is that it can cut down considerably on your work load and more than likely on your food costs. But it is not intended to short-change family appetites.

Incidentally, hearty eaters can finish up a whole casserole while others may just nibble. When planning a one-dish meal, it helps to overestimate: for six, cook enough for eight. If you're the cook you think you are, there will probably be calls for second helpings, anyway.

One-dish meals are a boon to all cooks, but especially to the beginner. They are designed to be easy to prepare, impressive to look at, and good to eat. The uncertain newlywed, about to entertain her in-laws for the first time, could do no better than to choose a Beef Ragout or a Chicken Potpie. Served in the elegant ambience of wedding-gift crystal, silver candelabra, and Madeira linen, the savory masterpiece is bound to convince any mother that her son is indeed a lucky man.

To cooks who make the mistake of putting too much food on the table, casseroles act as a sensible control. Too much of everything at a meal is an uneasy situation at best. Guests feel uncomfortable at the sight of untouched food. So does the hostess who hurries it out of sight as though it were testimony to her failure as a cook.

This casserole calculus works in reverse, too. We've all had the experience of dining with the optimist who plans to feed eight with a three-pound roast chicken. That same chicken, though, tucked in a hot pot with vegetables and a sauce, can save the day for all concerned.

We still remember the first formal meal we personally served to company. There were hors d'oeuvres, hot and cold, onion soup, roast beef, baked potatoes, two kinds of vegetables, tossed salad, caraway bread, and cherry pie and ice cream. The guests fled home, wearing puffy expressions; the hostess collapsed when she saw the pile of dishes to be washed in her pullman-kitchen sink. Contrast that with a Friday-night supper served to eight recently by a much wiser hostess: a simple but hearty fish chowder, mixed-greens salad, French bread, and lime sherbet. This time the guests were so content, they lingered to help with the dishes. Now there's another bonus when you choose one-dish meals—fewer dishes to do afterward!

It was only natural that in this streamlined world, cooks and hostesses would get around to streamlining their efforts. How much more agreeable when planning a meal to count to one—and stop right there. And don't think for a moment that one-dish meals are eternally casseroles. It's not necessarily so. They can be hearty soups—the kind the spoon stands straight up in, if you like them thick—or goulashes, stews, or ragouts (we'll explain *that* difference later), or appetizing salads—green, fruit, or molded—or hot pots, meat pies, and many, many more. Read on and see for yourself. We think you'll agree with us that the one-dish meal is more than a mathematical miracle. It's a whole chapter in gastronomical history.

I

Obviously, Casseroles

❁ ❁ ❁

When you're talking about one-dish meals, the obvious example is the casserole.

It is the epitome of everything a meal in one dish should be. Elaborate or simple. Hearty or delicately tempting. Easy to make and serve. Economical. There's no end of nice things to say about cooking under cover.

But like the nursery-rhyme girl with the curl in the middle of her forehead, when casseroles are good, they are delicious, and when they are bad, they are disgraceful.

We have been at parties where it has been impossible to identify the contents of the dinner casserole. At one we recall, the misguided hostess, in an effort to show off some new Mexican pottery, had put together an insipid mixture of odds and ends, drowning them in a coalescent sauce. It's concoctions such as this that give casseroles a bad name, particularly with the male sex. Men often get the same uncomfortable look on their faces when you say "casserole supper" as they do when you ask them to take out the garbage. May we ask all our readers

5

to take a pledge right now never to serve a casserole dish that requires a formal introduction. When the lid is lifted, it should at least be apparent that poultry, meat, or fish is involved.

This is not to say you shouldn't use leftovers in a casserole. After all, one of the great joys of this form of cookery is the way it disguises leftovers. But they should always be used with imagination and discretion. Reheated, tasteless ingredients buried in gravy are not the answer. What's more, it's important to consider flavors and textures when creating casseroles. Whatever you do, don't combine two or three foods that are natural enemies in your effort to get dinner to the table without much effort. Whether it's a spur-of-the-moment dish or a planned-weeks-in-advance meal, your casserole dinner should always advance your reputation as a good cook, not tarnish it.

Perhaps the casserole did originate for reasons of convenience and economy but it has certainly grown in stature over the years. Now it is considered suitable for practically any dining occasion. On the society page of a New York newspaper, we read the account of an al fresco wedding held in a field of flowers. The bride and her groom later presided at a bountiful wedding banquet—a huge casserole of beef balls and noodles that the bride had prepared the day before. With French bread, a green salad, and wine, it was a wedding feast to remember.

Casseroles—meaning the containers themselves—haven't stood still, either. Four hundred years ago or so, French cooks used to stew meat and vegetables in a large pot known as a *casse.* When families began making smaller amounts in individual containers, they dubbed them *casse-roles* or "little *casses."* Visit any housewares department today and you will marvel at what's happened to the "little *casse."* It is available in all sizes, shapes, and materials: glass, earthenware, aluminum, stainless steel, copper, pottery, porcelain over metal, iron. Glazed, heatproof, shatterproof. And in all colors of the rainbow.

For best results with casseroles, there are certain things you should know about the baking dish you select. It should be of the size and shape specified in the recipe. If you use a dish that is too large, the moisture will evaporate. If it's not big enough, the ingredients will probably bubble over and gum up both the pot and stove. If it is too deep a casserole, the food may undercook; too shallow, and it can overcook.

The intelligent solution is to have on hand an assortment of casseroles. Certainly three—large and deep, medium deep, and shallow. And make certain the covers fit tightly. You can always improvise a cover with heavy-duty foil if necessary. The shapes and colors you choose for your table can be as individual as you like. In fact, casserole meals, particularly buffets, offer an unlimited opportunity for you to demonstrate your skill at creating an elegant table setting.

If you're planning to try a new casserole recipe for a party, practice ahead of time to be certain that all will go well. (Warning: Always preheat the oven to the temperature specified in the recipe. Don't pop a casserole into a cold oven.) Besides, trying out a new recipe on the family first means you'll get an honest opinion about its tastiness. They may vote for a return to an old favorite. Oddly enough, it's often the simplest foods that perform best *en casserole*. Which, to our way of thinking, is another charming characteristic of this culinary art.

As a casserole devotee, you'll find it helpful to keep certain basic supplies on hand. Canned condensed cream of mushroom soup, cream of celery soup, and beef and chicken stock are virtual necessities. So are frozen chopped onions and green pepper, which will cut down on dicing and chopping time. Freeze-dried mushrooms and grated Parmesan cheese are two more habitués of the casserole scene. So are many herbs and seasonings, which should be purchased in small quantities and replaced often, since they are quick to lose their true flavor.

A time-saving trick that works nicely with casseroles is to double the recipe. Make twice the quantity your recipe calls for and bake in two casseroles, lining one in foil. The food cooked in foil will go into the freezer for one of those "no time to cook but we've still got to eat" days. Cool and freeze the contents of this second casserole, lift out the contents and wrap them in heavy freezer foil, and return to the freezer. When you're ready to serve it, all you need do is remove the foil, put the frozen meal back into a casserole, and heat slowly.

You know, of course, that casseroles may be cooked on top of the stove as easily as in the oven. However, this method requires more careful attention to prevent overcooking or scorching as well as a somewhat shorter cooking time. Whichever method you choose, casserole cookery allows you much more freedom than most other methods of food preparation. You'll never have to linger over a casserole constantly, watching and listening to each bubble and gurgle, like a doting mother with her firstborn.

A final bit of advice: "Nothing improves a casserole like a little judicious neglect."

Beef and Eggplant Bake

2 tablespoons butter or margarine
⅓ cup chopped onion
1 clove garlic, mashed
1½ pounds ground chuck
3 cans (8-ounce size) tomato sauce
2 teaspoons dried oregano leaves
1 teaspoon dried basil leaves

⅛ teaspoon anise seed
1 eggplant (about 1¼ pounds)
2 eggs, slightly beaten
½ cup packaged dried bread crumbs
1 cup grated Parmesan cheese
About ⅔ cup salad oil
1 package (8 ounces) mozzarella cheese, sliced

1. In hot butter in large skillet, sauté onion, garlic, and chuck about 5 minutes. Add tomato sauce, oregano, basil, and anise; mix well. Simmer, stirring, 5 minutes. Set aside.

2. Meanwhile, preheat oven to 350° F. Lightly grease a 12- by 8- by 2-inch baking dish.

3. Wash eggplant; slice crosswise ¼ inch thick.

4. In pie plate, combine eggs and 1 tablespoon water; mix well. Also, in another pie plate, combine bread crumbs with ½ cup Parmesan cheese; mix well.

5. Dip eggplant slices into egg mixture, coating well; then into crumb mixture, coating evenly.

6. Sauté eggplant slices in a little hot oil until golden brown and crisp on both sides. Add more oil as needed.

7. Place a single layer of eggplant in bottom of prepared baking dish. Sprinkle with some of remaining Parmesan cheese; top with a few slices of mozzarella cheese; cover with tomato sauce. Repeat layering until all ingredients are used, making certain to cover top completely with mozzarella cheese.

8. Bake, uncovered, 20 minutes, or until cheese is melted and bubbly.

Makes 6 servings.

Hamburger-and-Noodle Casserole

1 pound ground chuck
½ teaspoon seasoned salt
⅛ teaspoon pepper
1 package (5¾ ounces) noodle-casserole mix
1 can (8¾ ounces) cream-style corn

1 can (8 ounces) small white onions
1 can (3 ounces) sliced mushrooms
2 teaspoons Worcestershire sauce
2 tablespoons chopped pimiento

1. Preheat oven to 375° F. Lightly grease a 1½-quart casserole.

2. In skillet, combine beef, seasoned salt, and pepper. Sauté beef, stirring, until brown—10 to 15 minutes.

3. In prepared casserole, combine noodles with sauce mix from package. Add beef mixture; toss lightly to mix well. Layer the corn over the top.

4. Drain onions and mushrooms, reserving liquid from each. Add enough water to combined liquids to measure 1¾ cups. Add Worcestershire sauce. Bring to boiling in small saucepan.

5. Slowly pour boiling liquid over beef-and-noodle casserole.

6. Spoon onions, mushrooms, and pimiento over top.

7. Bake, covered, about 30 minutes. Bake, uncovered, 15 minutes longer, or until noodles are tender.

Makes 6 servings.

Hamburger Stroganoff

2 pounds ground chuck
1½ teaspoons salt
½ teaspoon pepper
2 tablespoons butter or margarine
1½ cups finely chopped onion
½ pound fresh mushrooms, sliced
2 tablespoons flour

2 tablespoons lemon juice
1 tablespoon Worcestershire sauce
½ cup canned condensed beef bouillon, undiluted
1 tablespoon catsup
1 cup dairy sour cream

Hot rice or noodles

1. Lightly mix beef with 1 teaspoon salt and ¼ teaspoon pepper. Shape into 18 meatballs, about 2 inches in diameter.

2. In hot butter in 4-quart Dutch oven, brown meatballs well all over. With slotted spoon, remove meatballs, and set aside.

3. Add onion and mushrooms to drippings in Dutch oven; sauté 5 minutes. Remove from heat. Stir in flour, then ½ teaspoon salt, ¼ teaspoon pepper, the lemon juice, the Worcestershire sauce, bouillon, and catsup.

4. Cook, stirring frequently, until thickened—about 5 minutes. Return meatballs to Dutch oven; simmer, covered, 20 minutes.

5. Stir in sour cream; cook over low heat, stirring, 3 minutes, or until hot. Serve hot over noodles or rice.

Makes 6 servings.

Meatball Surprise

1 pound ground chuck
1 egg, slightly beaten
½ cup milk
¾ cup crushed corn chips
2½ teaspoons salt
2½ tablespoons flour
2 tablespoons salad oil
3 medium-size onions, sliced (2 cups)
1 clove garlic, crushed
2 tablespoons sugar

1 tablespoon chili powder
1 teaspoon ground cumin
1 teaspoon ground coriander
1 teaspoon dried oregano leaves
1 can (1 pound, 3 ounces) tomatoes, undrained
1 square unsweetened chocolate

3 cups cooked white rice

1. In large bowl, combine chuck, egg, milk, corn chips, and 1 teaspoon salt; mix lightly with fork until well combined. Refrigerate, covered, 1 hour.

2. Shape mixture into 20 meatballs. Roll meatballs, lightly, in 2 tablespoons flour, coating completely.

3. In hot oil in large, heavy skillet with tight-fitting lid, brown meatballs, a few at a time. Remove as they are browned. Pour off all but 2 tablespoons fat from skillet.

4. In same skillet, sauté onion and garlic, stirring occasionally, about 5 minutes, or until tender. Remove from heat.

5. Combine sugar, chili powder, cumin, coriander, oregano, 1½ teaspoons salt, and remaining flour. Stir into skillet along with tomatoes, chocolate, and 1 cup water, mixing well.

6. Bring mixture to boiling, stirring constantly. Reduce heat; simmer, covered and stirring occasionally, 30 minutes. Add meatballs; simmer, covered, 20 minutes. Uncover; simmer 10 minutes longer.

7. Serve meatballs over hot rice.

Makes 4 to 6 servings.

Spinach-Beef Casserole

2 tablespoons olive or salad oil
1 pound ground chuck
½ teaspoon pepper
1 can (6 ounces) sliced
   mushrooms, undrained
⅓ cup dry sherry
1 can (1 pound) stewed
   tomatoes, undrained

1 package (10 ounces) frozen
   chopped spinach, thawed
1 package (6 ounces) noodles
   Italiano
½ cup grated sharp Cheddar
   cheese
Grated Parmesan cheese

Parsley sprigs

1. Preheat oven to 375° F. Lightly grease a 2-quart casserole.

2. In hot oil in large skillet, sauté chuck until lightly browned.

3. Add pepper, mushrooms, sherry, tomatoes, and spinach; mix well.

4. Bring to boiling. Reduce heat; simmer, covered, 10 minutes. Remove from heat.

5. Add uncooked noodles and the sauce mix and cheese filling from the package. Mix well to combine.

6. Turn into prepared casserole. Sprinkle with Cheddar cheese.

7. Bake, uncovered, 25 minutes, or until noodles are tender.

8. Before serving, sprinkle top with Parmesan cheese. Garnish with parsley sprigs.

Makes 4 to 6 servings.

Layaway Beef Casserole

⅔ cup salad or olive oil
9 pounds beef chuck, cut into 1-inch cubes
3 pounds small white onions, peeled
½ cup unsifted all-purpose flour
2 tablespoons sugar
5 teaspoons salt
¼ teaspoon black pepper
¾ teaspoon dried thyme leaves

3 cans (1-pound size) Italian tomatoes, undrained
3 cups Burgundy
2 bay leaves
5 strips orange peel (each 2 by ½ inch)

6 pounds unpared small new potatoes

Chopped parsley

1. In an 8-quart heavy kettle, slowly heat about 2 tablespoons oil. Add beef cubes, about one-sixth at a time, and cook over high heat until well browned on all sides. Add more oil as needed. Set beef aside.

2. Add onions to kettle; cook, stirring, until slightly browned. Remove onions, and set aside.

3. Remove kettle from heat. Stir in flour, sugar, salt, pepper, and thyme. Gradually stir in tomatoes and Burgundy. Add bay leaves, orange peel, and the browned beef.

4. Bring to boiling, stirring occasionally. Reduce heat; simmer, covered, 1½ hours.

5. Add browned onions; continue cooking 40 minutes longer, or until beef and onions are tender.

6. To freeze beef mixture: Remove and discard bay leaves and orange strips. Divide beef mixture into thirds. Place each third (8 servings) in a foil-lined 2-quart casserole; fold foil over beef mixture. Freeze until solid. Then remove foil package from casserole, and overwrap in freezer-wrapping material. Seal; label, and return to freezer.

7. To serve: Remove overwrap and foil from packages of frozen beef, according to number of servings desired. Place each 8-serving package in a 3-quart casserole; bake in a 400° F. oven, covered, 1 hour.

8. Meanwhile, cook potatoes in 1 inch boiling water in medium-size saucepan, covered, 15 minutes. Drain. (Use 2 pounds potatoes for each

third of beef mixture.) Add to beef mixture, and bake 20 minutes longer, or until potatoes are tender.

9. Garnish with chopped parsley.

Makes 24 servings in all.

Stuffed-Pepper Casserole

6 medium-size green peppers (1½ pounds)	1 teaspoon dried basil leaves
	1 teaspoon dried oregano leaves
2 tablespoons butter or margarine, melted	2½ teaspoons salt
	½ teaspoon pepper
½ cup chopped onion	1 egg
½ cup chopped celery	1 teaspoon Worcestershire sauce
1 can (1 pound, 3 ounces) tomatoes, undrained	1½ pounds ground chuck
1 can (8 ounces) tomato sauce	1½ cups cooked white rice
1 clove garlic, crushed	

1. Cut off tops of peppers; remove ribs and seeds. Chop edible portion of tops; set aside. Wash peppers.

2. Place peppers in large kettle with 2 quarts salted water. Bring to boiling; cover; reduce heat, and simmer 5 minutes. Drain peppers; set aside.

3. In hot butter in medium-size skillet, sauté chopped green pepper, onion, and celery until tender—3 to 5 minutes.

4. Add tomatoes, tomato sauce, garlic, basil, oregano, 1½ teaspoons salt, and ¼ teaspoon pepper. Simmer, uncovered, 10 minutes.

5. Preheat oven to 350° F.

6. Meanwhile, in large mixing bowl, combine egg, remaining salt and pepper, and Worcestershire. Beat with spoon to blend.

7. Add chuck, rice, and 1 cup of tomato mixture, mixing well.

8. Stuff peppers with meat mixture. Place in 3-quart casserole. Pour remaining tomato mixture over peppers.

9. Bake, uncovered, 1 hour.

Makes 6 servings.

Beef with Peppers and Eggplant

Peppers and Eggplant

3 medium-size green peppers (1 pound)
1 medium-size eggplant (1 pound)
5 tablespoons olive or salad oil
1 cup thinly sliced onion
1 clove garlic, crushed
1 can (2 pounds, 3 ounces) tomatoes
2½ teaspoons salt
¼ teaspoon pepper

¼ teaspoon dried rosemary leaves
1 bay leaf

1 flank steak (2½ pounds)
1 tablespoon olive or salad oil
1 teaspoon lemon juice
1 teaspoon salt
⅛ teaspoon pepper
1 clove garlic, crushed

1 tablespoon chopped parsley

1. Prepare Peppers and Eggplant: Wash peppers. Halve; remove seeds and ribs. Cut lengthwise in ½-inch-wide strips.

2. Wash eggplant. Do not peel. Cut lengthwise into quarters; slice crosswise into ¼-inch-thick slices.

3. In 3 tablespoons hot oil in 5-quart Dutch oven or kettle, sauté green pepper, onion, and 1 clove garlic until onion is golden and pepper is soft—about 10 minutes. Remove to medium-size bowl.

4. In same kettle, sauté eggplant in 2 tablespoons oil, stirring occasionally, for 5 minutes.

5. Return pepper mixture to kettle. Add undrained tomatoes, 2½ teaspoons salt, ¼ teaspoon pepper, the rosemary, and bay leaf; simmer, covered, 30 minutes.

6. Trim excess fat from steak; wipe steak with damp paper towels.

7. Combine oil, lemon juice, 1 teaspoon salt, ⅛ teaspoon pepper, and the garlic.

8. Place steak on broiler rack; brush with half of oil mixture. Broil, 4 inches from heat, 5 minutes. Turn; brush with remaining oil mixture. Broil 4 to 5 minutes longer.

9. Slice very thinly on the diagonal and across the grain. Add to vegetable mixture; mix gently. Turn into heated shallow serving dish or baking dish. Sprinkle with parsley.

Makes 8 servings.

Note: If desired, prepare Peppers and Eggplant day before; refrigerate. Reheat to bubbling just before adding meat.

Fruited Beef Casserole

2 tablespoons butter or
  margarine
2 medium-size onions, sliced
2 pounds ground chuck
1 egg
¼ cup milk
2 slices white bread, cubed
¼ cup dried apricots, finely
  chopped
¼ cup dark raisins
12 blanched almonds, chopped
2 tablespoons sugar
1 tablespoon curry powder

2 tablespoons lemon juice
2 teaspoons salt
¼ teaspoon pepper
5 bay leaves

Topping

1 egg
¾ cup milk
¼ teaspoon turmeric

Hot cooked rice
Chutney

1. In hot butter in large skillet, sauté onion until golden—about 5 minutes. Add chuck, and sauté until browned. Remove from heat.

2. Preheat oven to 350° F.

3. In large bowl, combine 1 egg, ¼ cup milk, and the bread cubes, mashing bread with fork. Add apricots, raisins, almonds, sugar, curry, lemon juice, salt, and pepper; mix until well blended.

4. Add meat mixture; mix lightly with fork. Turn into 2½-quart casserole, spreading evenly. Press bay leaves into mixture.

5. Bake, uncovered, 30 minutes.

6. Meanwhile, make Topping: In small bowl, beat egg with milk and turmeric just until blended. Set aside.

7. Remove casserole from oven; discard bay leaves. Pour topping over meat mixture.

8. Bake 10 to 15 minutes, uncovered, or just until topping is set. Serve with rice and chutney.

Makes 8 servings.

Lamb Pilaf

3 tablespoons butter or
  margarine
1½ pounds shoulder or breast of
  lean lamb, cut in 1-inch cubes
1 large onion, thinly sliced

1½ cups raw regular white rice
2 teaspoons salt
Dash pepper
½ teaspoon dried oregano
2 tablespoons chopped parsley

1. In large, heavy skillet—one that has a well-fitting cover—heat 1 tablespoon butter. Add lamb, and brown well on all sides; remove from skillet as it browns.

2. Preheat oven to 350° F.

3. In same skillet, in 1 tablespoon hot butter, sauté onion slices until golden.

4. Add remaining butter and rice; cook, stirring, over medium heat about 2 minutes, or until rice is lightly browned.

5. Add browned meat to rice mixture. Mix in 3 cups water, the salt, pepper, and oregano.

6. Bake, covered, 50 minutes, or until lamb is tender. Before serving, sprinkle with chopped parsley.

Makes 4 to 6 servings.

Lamb-Chop-and-White-Bean Casserole

1 cup dried pea beans
1 tablespoon salad oil
2 cups sliced onion
1 clove garlic, split
1 can (8 ounces) tomato sauce
   with mushrooms
¾ cup dry white wine
1½ teaspoons salt

½ teaspoon dried rosemary
   leaves
⅛ teaspoon pepper
1 package (10 ounces) frozen
   cut green beans
6 double loin lamb chops (3
   pounds)

Chopped chives

1. Soak pea beans in 3 cups cold water overnight. (Or, in large saucepan, combine pea beans with 3 cups water; bring to boiling; simmer 2 minutes. Cover; remove from heat. Let stand 1 hour.)

2. In large saucepan, simmer beans in same liquid, covered, 1 hour, or until tender. Drain beans, reserving any liquid.

3. Preheat oven to 375° F.

4. In salad oil in large skillet, sauté onion and garlic until onion is soft and lightly golden. Discard garlic.

5. Add pea beans to sautéed onion. Stir in the tomato sauce, wine, salt, rosemary, and pepper. Add green beans; bring mixture to boiling, breaking green beans apart with a fork.

6. Turn bean mixture into a shallow 2-quart casserole. Place in oven.

7. In hot, heavy frying pan, brown chops well on both sides. Remove as browned. Arrange, overlapping, on beans.

8. Bake, uncovered, 35 to 40 minutes, or until chops are done. Add reserved bean liquid, if needed.

9. Sprinkle with chopped chives.

Makes 4 to 6 servings.

Lamb Specialty Casserole

2 tablespoons salad oil	1½ teaspoons curry powder
2 pounds lamb shoulder, cut in 1-inch cubes	¼ teaspoon pepper
	½ pound zucchini, sliced
2 medium-size onions, sliced	1 package (9 ounces) frozen artichoke hearts
1 clove garlic, crushed	
½ cup raw regular white rice	2 cans (1-pound size) tomatoes, undrained
1 pound potatoes, pared and very thinly sliced	
4 teaspoons salt	Chopped parsley

1. Preheat oven to 350° F. In hot oil in large skillet, sauté lamb cubes, one-third at a time, until browned well on all sides (takes about 20 minutes in all). Remove lamb as it browns.

2. Add onion and garlic to drippings in skillet; sauté until golden—about 5 minutes.

3. Return lamb cubes to skillet, mixing well.

4. In a 3-quart casserole, place in layers one-third of meat mixture, rice, potatoes, salt, curry, pepper, zucchini, artichoke hearts, and tomatoes. Repeat layering twice, with rest of these ingredients.

5. Bake, covered, 2 hours, or until lamb and potatoes are tender. To serve, sprinkle top with parsley.

Makes 6 to 8 servings.

Curried Lamb and Beans

2 cups dried pea beans	2 teaspoons salt
3 tablespoons salad oil	1 to 1½ tablespoons curry powder
2 pounds shoulder of lamb, cut into 1½-inch cubes	⅓ cup chopped chutney
½ cup sliced onion	

1. Wash beans; turn into medium-size bowl. Cover with cold water. Refrigerate, covered, overnight.

2. Next day, drain beans. In large saucepan, cover beans with 6 cups water; bring to boiling. Reduce heat; simmer, covered, 45 to 55 minutes, or until beans are tender.

3. Drain beans, reserving 2¼ cups cooking liquid.

4. Meanwhile, in hot oil in heavy skillet with tight-fitting lid, or in Dutch oven, brown meat well.

5. Remove meat. In same skillet, sauté onion until tender—about 5 minutes.

6. Return meat to skillet. Stir in reserved cooking liquid, the salt, and curry powder; simmer, covered, 45 minutes, stirring occasionally.

7. Add beans; simmer, covered, 30 minutes longer. Stir in chutney. Makes 6 servings.

Lamb and Vegetables

4   tablespoons olive oil
2   cups braised lamb, cut into 1½-inch pieces
2   teaspoons lemon juice
1   teaspoon finely chopped garlic
1   teaspoon finely chopped shallots or scallions
1   large green pepper, seeded and cut into 2-inch squares
4   medium-size leeks, with diameters no larger than 1 inch (white parts and an inch or so of stems)

2   small zucchini, cut into ¾-inch rounds
3-inch strip of orange peel
½   teaspoon salt
Freshly ground black pepper
4   medium-size tomatoes, cut into quarters

1   tablespoon parsley, finely chopped

1. In a 10-inch heavy frying pan or shallow flameproof casserole, heat the olive oil until it begins to smoke.

2. Add the lamb, and brown the pieces for 2 or 3 minutes, turning them constantly in the hot oil with a spoon.

3. Turn the heat down to moderate, and mix in the lemon juice, garlic, and chopped shallots or scallions. Cook for 1 or 2 minutes longer. Then add the green pepper, leeks, zucchini, orange peel, salt, and a few grindings of black pepper.

4. Cover the pan tightly, and let the vegetables and meat cook over moderate heat for about 10 minutes, or until the leeks and zucchini are tender but still slightly firm.

5. Add the tomatoes, and cook 5 minutes longer.

6. To serve, arrange the meat and vegetables on a heated platter; pour the pan juices over them, and sprinkle with the parsley.

Makes 4 servings.

Note: The charm of this dish is to have the vegetables decidedly undercooked, their fresh flavor supporting the fully cooked and browned lamb.

Veal-and-Noodle Casserole

⅓ cup flour
3¼ teaspoons salt
¼ teaspoon pepper
3 pounds stewing veal, cut in
  1½-inch cubes
⅓ cup salad oil
2½ to 3 tablespoons paprika
1 pound yellow onions, peeled
  and sliced
2 cans (10½-ounce size)
  condensed beef broth,
  undiluted

½ teaspoon Worcestershire
  sauce
12 small white onions, peeled (½
  pound)
6 carrots, pared and halved
  crosswise
½ package (8-ounce size) wide
  noodles
1 cup dairy sour cream

Chopped parsley

1. On waxed paper, combine flour, 2¼ teaspoons salt, and the pepper. Use to coat veal. Reserve remaining flour mixture.

2. In some of hot oil in Dutch oven, brown veal, a third at a time, adding oil as needed. Remove as browned.

3. Preheat oven to 350° F.

4. Stir paprika into drippings in Dutch oven. Add sliced onion, and sauté until tender—about 10 minutes. Remove from heat.

5. Stir in reserved flour mixture until well blended. Stir in beef broth, Worcestershire, white onions, carrots, the browned veal, and 1 teaspoon salt. Bake, covered, 1½ hours.

6. Meanwhile, cook noodles as package label directs. Add cooked noodles to Dutch oven; bake ½ hour longer.

7. Stir a little hot liquid from Dutch oven into sour cream. Gradually stir sour cream into veal mixture until well blended. Garnish with parsley.

Makes 6 to 8 servings.

Note: Bake in 3-quart casserole, if you prefer.

Pork-Chop-and-Rice Casserole

4 loin pork chops (1½ pounds)	¼ teaspoon saffron
½ cup chopped onion	⅛ teaspoon pepper
1½ cups canned beef bouillon, undiluted	1½ cups raw regular white rice
½ teaspoon paprika	2 pimientos, drained and cut into strips
1½ teaspoons salt	

1. Preheat oven to 350° F. Wipe chops with damp paper towels. Slowly heat large, heavy skillet. In hot skillet, brown chops well—about 10 minutes on each side. Remove to 2-quart casserole.

2. Drain all but about 1 tablespoon fat from skillet. Add onion; sauté until tender—about 5 minutes.

3. Add bouillon, 1 cup water, paprika, salt, saffron, and pepper; mix well.

4. Sprinkle uncooked rice over chops. Pour onion mixture over all; bake, covered, 40 to 50 minutes.

5. Add pimiento during last 10 minutes of baking. Chops should be tender and rice fluffy, with most of liquid absorbed.

Makes 4 servings.

Ham-Noodle Casserole

1 package (5 ounces) noodles	1 clove garlic, finely chopped
¼ cup butter or margarine	1 can (6 ounces) sliced mushrooms, drained
½ cup finely chopped onion	

1 can (1 pound) fully cooked
  ham
1 tablespoon flour
1 can (8 ounces) tomato sauce
¼ cup Burgundy

1 can (10½ ounces) condensed
  beef bouillon, undiluted
¼ teaspoon pepper
1 cup dairy sour cream

½ cup grated Parmesan cheese

1. Preheat oven to 375° F.
2. Meanwhile, cook noodles as package label directs; drain. Set aside.
3. In hot butter in large skillet, sauté onion, garlic, and mushrooms until tender—about 5 minutes.
4. Remove and discard gelatin and excess fat from ham. Dice ham. Add to onion mixture; heat, stirring, 5 minutes longer.
5. Remove from heat. Stir in flour, tomato sauce, Burgundy, bouillon, and pepper; simmer 10 minutes, stirring occasionally. Remove from heat. Stir in sour cream.
6. In lightly greased, 2-quart casserole, layer one-third noodles; top with one-third ham mixture. Repeat layering twice. Sprinkle top with cheese.
7. Bake, uncovered, 25 minutes.
Makes 6 servings.

Ham-and-Potato Casserole

1¼ cups milk
4 cups thinly sliced, pared
  potatoes (2 pounds)
2 tablespoons butter or
  margarine
1 medium-size onion, sliced
2 tablespoons flour
½ teaspoon salt
¼ teaspoon pepper

1 cup light cream
1 slice fully cooked ham, 1½
  inches thick (2½ pounds)
1 tablespoon prepared mustard
Pinch dried marjoram leaves
1 tablespoon light-brown sugar

Chopped parsley (optional)

1. In large saucepan, bring milk to boiling. Add sliced potato; boil gently 5 minutes. Drain, reserving milk from potato—there should be 1 cup.
2. Preheat oven to 325° F.

3. In hot butter in medium-size saucepan, sauté onion until tender. Stir in flour, salt, and pepper until well blended. Gradually stir in reserved hot milk and the cream; cook, stirring constantly, until thickened. Remove from heat.

4. Trim excess fat from ham. Place in 13- by 9- by 2-inch baking dish. Spread mustard evenly over ham; sprinkle with marjoram. Spoon potato around ham; pour sauce over potato. Cover dish with foil.

5. Bake, covered, 30 minutes. Remove foil; sprinkle ham with brown sugar, and blend it into mustard with a fork. Bake, uncovered, 30 minutes, or until ham is tender and potato starts to brown. Garnish with parsley, if desired.

Makes 6 servings.

Bacon-Apple-and-Potato Casserole

1 (1½-pound size) slab bacon
⅓ cup light-brown sugar, firmly packed
6 medium-size potatoes, pared and cut crosswise into thirds

4 medium-size apples, pared, halved, and cored
⅛ teaspoon salt
¾ cup orange juice

Parsley sprigs

1. Remove rind from bacon; cut bacon into 1-inch chunks. (If bacon is very salty, it may be necessary to soak it overnight in cold water to cover. Then drain bacon.)

2. Preheat oven to 375° F.

3. In skillet, over low heat, sauté bacon, turning on all sides, until browned all over, pouring off drippings as they accumulate.

4. Turn bacon into Dutch oven. Sprinkle with sugar.

5. Arrange potatoes and apples around bacon; sprinkle potatoes with salt.

6. Add orange juice and ½ cup water. Bake, covered, until potatoes are tender—about 1 hour and 20 minutes. During baking, baste potatoes and apples occasionally with pan juices. Remove cover for last 10 minutes of baking.

7. Serve bacon surrounded with potatoes and apples. Garnish with parsley. Serve with pan juices.

Makes 4 to 6 servings.

Bacon-and-Macaroni Casserole

1 package (8 ounces) elbow macaroni
1 pound sliced bacon
½ cup chopped onion
⅓ cup coarsely chopped green pepper
¾ cup grated sharp Cheddar cheese

1 can (10½ ounces) condensed tomato soup, undiluted
1 cup milk
2 tablespoons packaged dry bread crumbs
¼ teaspoon dried thyme leaves

Parsley sprigs

1. Preheat oven to 375° F. Lightly grease a 2-quart casserole.
2. Cook macaroni as package label directs; drain. Turn into prepared casserole.
3. In skillet, over low heat, sauté 6 bacon slices until almost crisp. Drain; roll each into a curl. Set aside.
4. Cut rest of bacon slices crosswise into ½-inch pieces. Sauté until almost crisp. Drain off all but 2 tablespoons drippings.
5. Add onion and green pepper to bacon in skillet; sauté until tender—about 5 minutes.
6. With slotted spoon, lift bacon and vegetables to casserole. Add ½ cup cheese. Toss all together to combine well.
7. Combine soup and milk. Pour over macaroni mixture; mix well. Arrange bacon curls on top.
8. Combine bread crumbs, thyme, and rest of cheese. Sprinkle over top of casserole.
9. Bake 25 to 30 minutes, or until bubbly and brown. Garnish with parsley.
   Makes 6 servings.

Macaroni-Chili Casserole

2 slices bacon, cut up
1½ pounds beef chuck or rump, cut in ½-inch cubes
1 cup sliced onion
1 can (1 pint, 2 ounces) tomato juice

1 envelope (1¼ ounces) chili-seasoning mix
1 can (15 ounces) red kidney beans, undrained
1 package (8 ounces) elbow macaroni
½ cup grated Cheddar cheese

1. In Dutch oven, fry bacon pieces until crisp. Remove pieces; reserve.

2. Add beef and onion to bacon fat, and sauté until well browned— about 15 minutes.

3. Add the tomato juice and chili-seasoning mix; bring to boiling. Reduce heat, and simmer, covered and stirring occasionally, 1 hour, or until beef is tender.

4. Add kidney beans; simmer 15 minutes longer. Meanwhile, cook macaroni as package label directs; drain. Stir into beef mixture with bacon. Turn into 2½-quart casserole; sprinkle with cheese. Broil, 4 inches from heat, until cheese melts.

Makes 6 to 8 servings.

Sausage-and-Rice Casserole

1 pound sausage meat	½ teaspoon salt
1 cup chopped onion	⅛ teaspoon pepper
1 cup chopped celery	2 teaspoons bottled thick steak
1 cup washed, sliced fresh	sauce
mushrooms	⅓ cup grated Parmesan cheese
1 cup raw regular white rice	¼ cup chopped pimiento
2 cups canned beef bouillon	

1. Preheat oven to 350° F.

2. In large skillet, sauté sausage, stirring, 5 minutes. Remove sausage with slotted spoon.

3. In drippings, sauté onion, celery, and sliced mushrooms, stirring, 5 minutes.

4. Add rice; sauté, stirring, 5 minutes longer. Turn into ungreased 2-quart casserole.

5. Heat bouillon to boiling. Add to rice mixture, along with sausage, salt, pepper, steak sauce, cheese, and pimiento; mix well.

6. Bake, covered, 1 hour, or until rice is tender.

Makes 4 to 6 servings.

Saturday Night Casserole

¼ cup salad oil
6 Italian sweet sausages (about 1¼ pounds)
2 cups uncooked elbow macaroni
1 pound ground chuck
1 can (6 ounces) tomato paste
2 cans (1-pound size) stewed tomatoes, undrained

1 can (8 ounces) tomato sauce with onion
1 tablespoon garlic salt
½ teaspoon pepper
1 tablespoon dried basil leaves
1 tablespoon dried oregano leaves
½ pound sliced Muenster cheese (optional)

1. In hot oil in electric skillet, set at 275° F., or in skillet over moderately high heat, brown sausage well on all sides.

2. Add macaroni and ground chuck; sauté, stirring, 5 minutes, or until beef loses its pink color.

3. Stir in tomato paste, stewed tomatoes, tomato sauce, garlic salt, pepper, basil, oregano, and 2½ cups water. Bring to boiling, stirring; reduce heat, and simmer, covered, 45 minutes.

4. Arrange cheese slices over top; heat just until cheese melts slightly. Makes 6 servings.

Chicken-and-Mushroom Casserole

¼ cup butter or margarine
8 chicken legs with thighs (3 pounds)
¼ cup flour
1 can (1 pound) whole onions, drained
1 can (4 ounces) chopped mushrooms, drained
1 small can evaporated milk, undiluted (⅔ cup)

1 can (10½ ounces) condensed cream of mushroom soup, undiluted
½ package (8-ounce size) sharp Cheddar cheese, grated (1 cup)
⅛ teaspoon pepper
Paprika

1. Preheat oven to 425° F. Melt butter in a 13- by 9- by 2-inch baking dish.

2. Wash chicken legs, and drain on paper towels. Coat completely with flour. Place, skin side down, in butter in pan.

3. Bake, uncovered, 30 minutes. Turn pieces; bake 15 to 20 minutes longer, or just until chicken is well browned. Remove from oven.

4. Reduce oven temperature to 325° F. Add onions and mushrooms.

5. In medium-size bowl, combine evaporated milk, soup, cheese, and pepper; mix until well blended. Pour over chicken and vegetables; sprinkle with paprika. Cover pan with foil.

6. Bake 15 to 20 minutes, or just until sauce is bubbly and hot. Makes 8 servings.

Chicken-and-Shrimp Casserole

1 pound raw shrimp, shelled and deveined	1 can (10½ ounces) condensed tomato soup, undiluted
2½ teaspoons salt	1 cup heavy cream
¾ cup raw regular white rice	½ cup dry sherry
2 chicken legs and thighs (1 pound)	½ teaspoon Worcestershire sauce
2 whole chicken breasts, split (1½ pounds)	¼ teaspoon pepper
	¼ teaspoon dried thyme leaves
3 tablespoons salad oil	
½ cup chopped onion	2 tablespoons chopped parsley
½ cup chopped green pepper	

1. In large saucepan, bring 1 quart water to boiling; add shrimp and 1 teaspoon salt. Return to boiling; reduce heat, and simmer, covered, 10 minutes. Drain.

2. Preheat oven to 350° F. Cook the rice as package label directs. Wash chicken, and pat dry with paper towels.

3. In hot oil in 4-quart Dutch oven, brown chicken well on all sides. Remove pieces as browned.

4. Discard all but 2 tablespoons drippings from Dutch oven. In hot drippings, sauté onion and green pepper until tender—about 5 minutes. Remove from heat.

5. Stir in soup, cream, sherry, 1½ teaspoons salt, the Worcestershire, pepper, and thyme until well blended. Add cooked rice, chicken, and shrimp.

6. Bake, covered, 60 minutes, or until chicken is tender. Sprinkle with parsley.

Makes 6 servings.

Note: If you prefer, brown the chicken, onion, and green pepper in a skillet; then combine with other ingredients (see Step 5) in 3-quart casserole.

Chicken-Tomato Casserole

1 (4-pound size) roasting chicken, cut up
2 tablespoons butter or margarine
2 tablespoons olive or salad oil
1 large onion, sliced
1 large carrot, sliced
1 stalk celery, sliced
1 can (1 pound) Italian tomatoes, undrained
1 tablespoon dried basil leaves

1 tablespoon dried oregano leaves
1½ teaspoons salt
¼ teaspoon cinnamon
⅛ teaspoon black pepper
4 whole cloves
½ cup dry white wine
¼ pound fresh mushrooms, washed and sliced
1 tablespoon flour

1. Wash chicken; pat dry with paper towels.

2. Heat butter and oil in 4-quart Dutch oven. Add chicken, a few pieces at a time, and brown well on all sides. Remove as browned, and set aside.

3. Add onion, carrot, and celery to Dutch oven, and sauté until golden—about 5 minutes. Add tomatoes, basil, oregano, salt, cinnamon, pepper, and cloves; mix well, mashing tomatoes with fork.

4. Bring to boiling; reduce heat, and simmer, uncovered, 10 minutes.

5. Add browned chicken and the wine; simmer, covered, for 50 to 60 minutes, or until chicken is tender. Add mushrooms; cook, uncovered, 10 minutes longer.

6. Remove chicken to a warm, deep dish. Dissolve flour in 2 tablespoons water; stir into sauce; bring to boiling, stirring until thickened. Pour over chicken.

Makes 6 servings.

Chicken-and-Vegetables Casserole

1 (4-pound size) ready-to-cook roasting chicken, cut in serving pieces

1 slice bacon
1 tablespoon salt
¼ teaspoon pepper

4 small yellow onions, peeled
and quartered

4 carrots, pared and cut in
2-inch pieces

2 white turnips, pared and cut
in 2-inch cubes

2 stalks celery, cut in 1-inch
pieces

1 green pepper, cut in strips

1 can (6 ounces) whole
mushrooms, undrained

3 medium-size tomatoes, halved

2 bay leaves

1 teaspoon dried rosemary
leaves

Parsley sprigs (optional)

1. Preheat oven to 375° F. Wash chicken, and dry with paper towels.

2. Lay bacon in bottom of a 4-quart casserole. Place chicken on bacon. Sprinkle with some of the salt and pepper.

3. Arrange vegetables in layers in casserole, ending with tomatoes. Push bay leaves down into vegetables; sprinkle with rosemary and remaining salt and pepper.

4. Bake, covered, 1 hour and 50 minutes, or until chicken and vegetables are tender. Bring some chicken pieces up to surface before serving. Garnish with parsley sprigs, if desired.

Makes 6 to 8 servings.

Party Tetrazzini

2 pounds whole chicken
breasts, split

3 pounds chicken legs and
thighs

3 celery tops

3 parsley sprigs

2 medium-size carrots, pared
and sliced

1 medium-size onion, quartered

2 teaspoons salt

10 whole black peppercorns

1 bay leaf

Sauce

¾ cup butter or margarine

¾ cup all-purpose flour

3 teaspoons salt

⅛ teaspoon nutmeg

Dash cayenne

1 quart milk

4 egg yolks

1 cup heavy cream

½ cup dry sherry

1 package (1 pound) thin
spaghetti

2 cans (6-ounce size) whole
mushrooms, drained

2 packages (8-ounce size) sharp
Cheddar cheese, grated (4
cups)

1. Wash chicken. Place in 6-quart kettle with 3 cups water, the celery, parsley, carrots, onion, salt, peppercorns, and bay leaf. Bring to boiling; reduce heat, and simmer, covered, 1 hour, or until chicken is tender.

2. Remove chicken from stock to bowl; set aside. Strain stock; return to kettle. Bring to boiling; boil gently, uncovered, until reduced to 2 cups—about 30 minutes.

3. Remove chicken meat from bones in large pieces—there should be about 6 cups. Set the chicken meat aside.

4. Make Sauce: Melt butter in large saucepan. Remove from heat. Stir in flour, salt, nutmeg, and cayenne until smooth. Gradually stir in milk and the 2 cups stock; bring to boiling, stirring constantly. Boil gently, stirring constantly, 2 minutes, or until slightly thickened.

5. In small bowl, beat egg yolks with cream. Gently beat in a little of the hot mixture. Add egg-yolk mixture to saucepan; cook over low heat, stirring constantly, until sauce is hot—do not let it boil. Remove from heat. Add sherry.

6. Cook spaghetti as package label directs; drain. Return spaghetti to kettle. Add 2 cups sauce, and toss until well blended.

7. Remove another 2 cups sauce, and refrigerate, covered. To remaining sauce, add cut-up chicken and the mushrooms.

8. Divide spaghetti into two 12- by 8- by 2-inch baking dishes, arranging it around edges. Spoon half of chicken mixture into center of each. Sprinkle 2 cups cheese over spaghetti in each dish. Cover with foil; refrigerate.

9. About 1 hour before serving, preheat oven to 350° F. Bake, covered, 30 to 45 minutes, or until piping hot.

10. Just before serving reheat reserved sauce, and spoon over spaghetti in baking dishes.

Makes 12 servings.

Turkey Tetrazzini

Sauce

½ cup butter or margarine	Dash nutmeg
½ cup all-purpose flour	Dash cayenne
1½ teaspoons salt	2 cups milk

1   can (10½ ounces) condensed chicken broth
2   egg yolks
½   cup light cream
¼   cup dry sherry

1   package (8 ounces) thin spaghetti

4   cups cooked turkey, in large pieces
1   can (6 ounces) sliced mushrooms
1   cup grated sharp Cheddar cheese

1. Make Sauce: Melt butter in medium-size saucepan. Remove from heat. Stir in flour, salt, nutmeg, and cayenne until smooth. Gradually stir in milk and undiluted chicken broth; bring to boiling, stirring constantly. Boil gently, stirring constantly, 2 minutes, or until slightly thickened.

2. In small bowl, beat egg yolks with cream. Gently beat in a little of hot mixture. Return to saucepan; cook over low heat, stirring constantly, until sauce is hot—do not let it boil. Remove from heat. Add sherry.

3. Preheat oven to 350° F.

4. Cook spaghetti in kettle as package label directs; drain. Return spaghetti to kettle. Add 2 cups sauce, and toss until well blended.

5. Add turkey and mushrooms to the remaining sauce.

6. Turn spaghetti into a 12- by 8- by 2-inch baking dish. Spoon turkey mixture over top. Sprinkle with cheese.

7. Bake, covered, 25 to 30 minutes, or until piping hot.

Makes 8 servings.

Seafood Casserole

2   packages (6-ounce size) wild-and-white-rice mix
1   pound Oregon Dungeness crab, cooked and cleaned, or 2 cans (7¾-ounce size) king-crab meat, drained
4   cans (4½-ounce size) shrimp, drained

3   cans (10½-ounce size) condensed cream of mushroom soup, undiluted
⅓   cup grated onion
1   cup chopped green pepper
1   cup chopped celery
1   jar (4 ounces) pimiento, drained and chopped
2   tablespoons lemon juice

1. Cook wild-and-white-rice mix as package label directs.
2. Remove any cartilage from crab meat. Rinse shrimp in cold water, and drain again.
3. Preheat oven to 325° F. Lightly grease a 4-quart casserole. Combine all ingredients right in casserole, and stir to mix well. (If desired, reserve a little shrimp and crab meat to garnish top of casserole.)
4. Bake, uncovered, 1 hour.
Makes 10 to 12 servings.

Creole Jambalaya

2 tablespoons butter or margarine
½ cup chopped onion
1 clove garlic, crushed
¼ pound cooked ham, diced (¾ cup)
1 can (1 pound) tomatoes, undrained
¾ cup canned condensed chicken broth

1½ pounds raw shrimp, shelled and deveined
1 tablespoon chopped parsley
1 bay leaf
1 teaspoon salt
¼ teaspoon dried thyme leaves
½ teaspoon Tabasco
⅛ teaspoon pepper
1 cup raw long-grain white rice

1. Preheat oven to 350° F.
2. In hot butter in 4-quart Dutch oven, sauté onion until soft—about 5 minutes. Add garlic and ham; sauté 5 minutes longer.
3. Stir in tomatoes, chicken broth, shrimp, parsley, bay leaf, salt, thyme, Tabasco, and pepper. Bring to boiling, covered.
4. Pour into a 2-quart casserole. Sprinkle rice over top of mixture; gently press into liquid just until rice is covered—do not stir. Cover.
5. Bake 40 minutes, or until rice is tender and liquid is absorbed. Toss gently before serving.
Makes 6 servings.

Rice with Clams and Shrimp

Fried Eggplant (see p. 32)
1 dozen small clams, in shell

2 pounds raw shrimp, shelled and deveined

4 tablespoons olive or salad oil	2 green peppers, seeded and
1 tablespoon butter or	finely chopped
margarine	4 large tomatoes, peeled
1 cup raw long-grain white rice	½ cup pimiento-stuffed olives,
1 teaspoon salt	sliced
1 bay leaf	2 teaspoons paprika
1 chicken-bouillon cube	⅛ teaspoon cayenne
2 cloves garlic, finely chopped	1½ cups (6 ounces) grated
2 medium-size onions, peeled	Cheddar cheese
and finely chopped	

1. Prepare Fried Eggplant.

2. Wash clams and shrimp thoroughly. Place clams in saucepan with 6 cups water; bring to boiling. Add shrimp; cook over high heat, covered, 5 minutes. Remove from heat.

3. Pour off enough shellfish liquid to make 2¼ cups. Set aside clams and shrimp in remaining broth; keep warm.

4. Heat 2 tablespoons olive oil and the butter in 3-quart saucepan. Add rice, and stir to coat well. Add reserved 2¼ cups liquid, the salt, bay leaf, and bouillon cube. Bring to boiling; lower heat, and simmer, covered and without stirring, 25 minutes.

5. Preheat oven to 375° F. Meanwhile, in 2 tablespoons hot oil in 6-quart Dutch oven, sauté garlic, onion, and green pepper until green pepper is tender—about 10 minutes.

6. Chop 2 tomatoes. Add to sautéed vegetables with olives, paprika, and cayenne; cook 5 minutes longer. Keep warm.

7. Drain shellfish, and add with rice to tomato mixture; stir gently to blend. Turn into paella pan or shallow 4-quart casserole.

8. Slice 2 remaining tomatoes, and arrange around edge of dish alternately with Fried Eggplant. Sprinkle cheese over top of all. Bake 10 to 15 minutes, uncovered, or until cheese is melted and bubbly.

Makes 6 to 8 servings.

Fried Eggplant

1 small eggplant (1 pound)	1 cup packaged dry bread
2 teaspoons salt	crumbs
2 eggs, beaten	Olive or salad oil

1. About 4 hours before cooking, cut eggplant into strips ½ inch thick. Sprinkle with salt. Place in strainer, in bowl, and set aside.

2. When ready to cook, dip each piece of eggplant into beaten egg; then roll in bread crumbs.

3. Heat oil (1 inch deep) in large skillet to 375° F. on deep-frying thermometer.

4. Drop eggplant, several pieces at a time, into hot oil, and cook, turning once, until nicely browned on both sides—about 2 minutes.

5. Lift out with slotted utensil, and drain on paper towels. Keep warm.

Makes 6 to 8 servings.

Sole-Florentine Casserole

1 can (10 ounces) frozen cream of shrimp soup
2 pounds fillets of sole
2 tablespoons butter or margarine
½ teaspoon salt
2 packages (10-ounce size) frozen chopped spinach

3 tablespoons dry sherry
1 tablespoon butter or margarine, melted
3 tablespoons packaged dry bread crumbs
2 tablespoons grated Parmesan cheese

1. Preheat oven to 350° F. Thaw soup as package label directs.

2. Wash sole; drain on paper towels. Fold fillets in half crosswise; arrange in a single layer in a 12- by 8- by 2-inch baking dish.

3. Dot fish with 2 tablespoons butter; sprinkle with salt. Pour on ½ cup water.

4. Cover dish with foil; bake 20 minutes.

5. Meanwhile, cook spinach as the package label directs. Drain very well.

6. Also, in medium-size saucepan, heat cream of shrimp soup to boiling. Stir in sherry.

7. Remove fish from baking dish; discard liquid. Spread spinach over bottom of dish; top with fillets of sole. Pour shrimp-soup mixture over fish.

8. Combine melted butter with bread crumbs and cheese; sprinkle over top.

9. Bake, uncovered, 20 minutes.

Makes 6 servings.

Curried-Lobster Casserole

4   (8-ounce size) frozen lobster
    tails
1   package (7 ounces) frozen
    Chinese pea pods
1   package (1½ ounces)
    curry-sauce mix
½   cup mayonnaise
1   can (5 ounces) water
    chestnuts, drained and sliced

1   tablespoon butter or
    margarine
1   can (4½ ounces) blanched
    whole almonds

Hot cooked fluffy white rice
Prepared chutney

1. Add lobster to lightly salted, boiling water to cover. Bring back to boiling; reduce heat, and simmer, uncovered, 5 minutes; drain, reserving 1¾ cups liquid. Remove lobster meat from shell.

2. Halve lobster meat lengthwise; then cut the meat crosswise into ½-inch pieces.

3. Cook pea pods as package label directs; drain.

4. Preheat oven to 375° F.

5. Make curry sauce as package label directs, using reserved lobster liquid. Bring to boiling. Remove from heat. Blend in mayonnaise.

6. In a 1½-quart casserole, combine lobster, pea pods, water chestnuts, and curry sauce; mix well. Bake, uncovered, 20 minutes.

7. Meanwhile, in hot butter, sauté almonds, stirring, until browned—about 5 minutes. Spoon almonds over top of casserole.

8. Serve lobster over white rice, along with chutney.

Makes 6 servings.

Tuna Casserole with Almonds

3   quarts boiling water
Salt
1   package (8 ounces)
    medium-size noodles
2   cans (10½-ounce size)
    condensed cream of celery
    soup, undiluted
⅔   cup dry sherry
3   tablespoons chopped parsley

1   teaspoon instant minced
    onion
¾   teaspoon dried marjoram
    leaves
3   cans (7-ounce size)
    chunk-style tuna, drained
½   cup toasted sliced almonds
3   tablespoons butter or
    margarine, melted

1. Preheat oven to 350° F. Lightly grease a 2½-quart casserole.
2. In 3 quarts boiling, salted water, cook noodles, uncovered, 8 minutes, or until just tender; drain.
3. In large bowl; combine soup, sherry, parsley, onion, marjoram, 1 teaspoon salt, the tuna, and noodles; toss to mix well. Turn into prepared casserole.
4. Toss almonds with melted butter; sprinkle over top of casserole.
5. Bake 35 to 40 minutes, uncovered, or until mixture is bubbly.
Makes 8 servings.

Tuna and Eggplant Parmigiana

Tomato Sauce

2 tablespoons butter or margarine
½ cup chopped onion
1 clove garlic, crushed
1 can (1 pound) Italian tomatoes, undrained
1 can (8 ounces) tomato sauce
1 tablespoon sugar
¼ teaspoon salt
¼ teaspoon Italian seasoning

¼ cup flour

¼ teaspoon salt
⅛ teaspoon pepper
1 medium-size eggplant (about 1¼ pounds)
⅓ cup salad oil
2 cans (6½-ounce size) chunk-style tuna, drained and flaked
¼ cup grated Parmesan cheese
½ package (8-ounce size) mozzarella cheese, sliced

1. Make Tomato Sauce: In hot butter in medium-size saucepan, sauté onion and garlic until onion is golden brown—about 5 minutes. Add tomatoes, tomato sauce, sugar, ¼ teaspoon salt, and the Italian seasoning; bring to boiling. Reduce heat, and simmer, uncovered and stirring frequently, 20 minutes—there should be about 3 cups.
2. Meanwhile, on sheet of waxed paper, combine flour, ¼ teaspoon salt, and the pepper. Wash eggplant; cut crosswise into ½-inch-thick slices. Dip slices into flour mixture, coating both sides.
3. Heat about 2 tablespoons oil in skillet. Add eggplant, a few slices at a time, and sauté until golden brown on each side. Remove eggplant as it browns. Add more oil as needed.

4. Preheat oven to 350° F.

5. Spoon half of sauce into an 8- by 8- by 2-inch or a 9-inch round baking dish. Place half of eggplant in sauce; top with tuna, then remaining eggplant. Spoon remaining sauce over top. Sprinkle with Parmesan cheese; then top with mozzarella slices.

6. Bake, uncovered, 30 minutes, or just until cheese is melted and golden.

Makes 6 servings.

Tuna-and-Vegetable Casserole

1 can (8½ ounces) peas
1 can (10½ ounces) condensed Cheddar cheese soup, undiluted
2 cans (7-ounce size) tuna, drained and flaked
1 can (1 pound) julienne carrots, drained

2 hard-cooked eggs, sliced
1 can (15 ounces) macaroni and cheese
½ teaspoon dried rosemary leaves
⅛ teaspoon pepper
1 can (3½ ounces) French-fried onion rings

1. Preheat oven to 350° F. Lightly grease a 2-quart casserole.

2. Drain peas, reserving ⅓ cup liquid.

3. In small saucepan, combine reserved liquid from peas with cheese soup; mix well.

4. Bring to boiling, over medium heat, stirring constantly.

5. In prepared casserole, layer half the tuna, carrots, peas, egg slices, and macaroni and cheese; sprinkle with half the rosemary and pepper.

6. Spoon half the cheese-soup mixture over tuna and vegetables. Repeat layering, topping with rest of soup mixture.

7. Bake 25 minutes, uncovered, or until hot and bubbly. Sprinkle top with fried onion rings. Bake 5 minutes longer.

Makes 6 servings.

Tuna Tetrazzini

7 tablespoons butter or margarine
½ pound fresh mushrooms, washed and sliced

½ package (1-pound size) large shell macaroni
¼ cup unsifted all-purpose flour
1 teaspoon salt

½ teaspoon dry mustard
⅛ teaspoon pepper
2 cups milk
½ cup dry sherry
1 package (8 ounces) sharp
Cheddar cheese, grated

3 cans (7-ounce size) tuna,
drained

Buttered peas (optional)
Marinated cucumber slices
(optional)

1. Preheat oven to 375° F.
2. In 3 tablespoons hot butter in medium-size skillet, sauté mushrooms 5 minutes, stirring occasionally.
3. Cook macaroni as package directs; drain.
4. Melt remaining butter in medium-size saucepan. Remove from heat. Stir in flour, salt, mustard, pepper. Gradually stir in milk and sherry.
5. Bring to boiling, stirring. Remove from heat. Add 1½ cups cheese; stir until melted.
6. In a 2-quart casserole, combine tuna, mushrooms, macaroni, and cheese sauce. Sprinkle remaining cheese over top.
7. Bake, uncovered, 20 to 25 minutes, or until golden and bubbly. Serve for supper, with buttered peas and marinated cucumber slices, if desired.
Makes 8 servings.

Cheese Casserole

2 cans (4-ounce size) green
chilies, drained
1 pound Monterey Jack cheese,
coarsely grated
1 pound Cheddar cheese,
coarsely grated
4 egg whites, at room
temperature
4 egg yolks

⅔ cup canned evaporated milk,
undiluted
1 tablespoon flour
½ teaspoon salt
⅛ teaspoon pepper
2 medium-size tomatoes, sliced

Chopped green chilies (optional)

1. Preheat oven to 325° F. Remove seeds from chilies, and dice.
2. In a large bowl, combine the grated cheese and green chilies. Turn into a well-buttered, shallow 2-quart casserole (12 by 8 by 2 inches).

3. In large bowl, with electric mixer at high speed, beat egg whites just until stiff peaks form when beater is slowly raised.

4. In small bowl of electric mixer, combine egg yolks, evaporated milk, flour, salt, and pepper; mix until well blended.

5. Using a rubber scraper, gently fold beaten whites into egg-yolk mixture.

6. Pour egg mixture over cheese mixture in casserole, and using a fork, "ooze" it through the cheese.

7. Bake 30 minutes, uncovered; remove from oven, and arrange sliced tomatoes, overlapping, around edge of casserole. Bake 30 minutes longer, or until a silver knife inserted in center comes out clean. Garnish with a sprinkling of chopped green chilies, if desired.

Makes 6 to 8 servings.

Corn Casserole

1 large eggplant	4 cups fresh corn kernels, cut
3 large tomatoes	from cob
½ cup unsifted all-purpose flour	¼ cup packaged dry bread
Salt	crumbs
Pepper	½ cup grated Parmesan cheese
1 cup salad oil	¼ cup butter or margarine
1 small Bermuda onion, thinly	
sliced	

1. Preheat oven to 400° F. Lightly grease a 12- by 8- by 2-inch baking dish.

2. Cut eggplant and tomatoes into ½-inch-thick slices.

3. Combine flour, 1 teaspoon salt, ¼ teaspoon pepper. Coat eggplant and tomatoes with flour mixture.

4. In a large, heavy skillet, heat half of oil.

5. In the hot oil, sauté eggplant and tomato slices, a few at a time, until browned on both sides; remove slices as they brown. Add more oil to skillet as needed.

6. In prepared dish, layer half of eggplant, tomato, onion, and corn. Repeat.

7. Sprinkle with salt and pepper.

8. Toss bread crumbs and cheese. Sprinkle over vegetables. Dot with butter.

9. Bake, covered, 20 minutes. Uncover; bake 20 minutes longer. Makes 8 servings.

Lima-Bean Casserole

1 package (1 pound) large dried lima beans	2 tablespoons butter or margarine
½ cup finely chopped carrot	2 tablespoons salad oil
1 cup finely chopped onion	1 clove garlic, finely chopped
1 cup finely chopped celery	Pinch dried thyme leaves
2 cups finely chopped tomato	1 teaspoon dry mustard
2 teaspoons salt	1 teaspoon paprika
¼ teaspoon pepper	2 tablespoons dry white wine

1. Cover beans with cold water; refrigerate, covered, overnight. Next day, drain. Turn into large kettle.

2. Add carrot, onion, celery, tomato, salt, pepper, and 3 cups cold water. Bring to boiling point; reduce heat, and simmer, covered, 1 hour; stir frequently.

3. Drain beans; discard liquid.

4. Meanwhile, preheat oven to 300° F. Turn bean mixture into 2-quart casserole.

5. Stir in butter, salad oil, garlic, thyme, mustard, and paprika; bake, covered, 2 hours, or until beans are tender (stir several times during baking, so beans cook evenly).

6. Just before serving, stir in white wine.

Makes 6 servings.

II

Soups Can Do It

❁ ❁ ❁

Soup was not always regarded as something with which to keep people occupied at the dining table while out in the kitchen the cook struggles to assemble the main course.

Soup *was* the main course, once upon a time. In fact, the word *supper* comes from *la soupe,* the name given to the evening meal in rural areas of France. There was a time in culinary history when bowls of broth filled with meat or vegetables comprised the meal. However, as people became more cultured, menus became more sophisticated. Soup was labeled peasant fare and diners scorned it.

Eventually, when soup was restored to favor, it had a new guise. It no longer was the meal itself, but rather an appetite teaser. The idea caught on and famous chefs outdid themselves creating new and fancy varieties of bouillons, broths, purees, and bisques to stimulate jaded palates.

Today, soups have come full cycle. It is quite acceptable again to use them as main courses, accompanied by a salad and a light dessert.

As a main course, soup can have as many charms as a rich bachelor. Obviously, it can be nutritious, easy to make, and thrifty. It can also bring glamour and charm to what might otherwise be an ordinary meal. There are soups that evoke distant countries, like the pot-au-feu of France, the Borsch of Russia, the minestrone of Italy. There are soups

40

that stimulate not only the appetite but conversation as well, if one knows their history. Gumbo soup, for example, has a fascinating story behind it. Created by the emigré French, or Creoles as they were known in New Orleans, the secret of its special flavor came from "filé," a seasoning made from the leaves of sassafras trees. And who told the newcomers about filé? The Choctaw Indians who had preceded them in Louisiana. Today filé is difficult to obtain and you may have to replace it with okra when you make your gumbo. In New Orleans that version is called the "lazy man's gumbo."

Your diet-conscious friends, in particular, will glow when you announce the main course is soup. "There's something so skinny about eating soup," a heavyweight friend once commented. "Maybe lobster bisque and corn chowder do have loads of calories, but the fact doesn't register the way it does when I come face to face with fried chicken and potato salad!"

If you're eager to try soup as a main course, start out with some of the heavier soups first, such as Lentil Soup with Ham or fish chowder. Having convinced the members of your family that soup can be as satisfying as a three-course meal, you can go on to experiment with other more exotic varieties. In most instances, you'll want to round out the meal with compatible "accessories," such as a crisp green salad, rolls, and an assortment of cheese. You'll discover that soup meals are particularly suitable for brunches and suppers. It's true, of course, that both Queen Elizabeth I and Queen Victoria enjoyed a bowl of mutton soup for breakfast every day—but better not try to push your luck that far.

It also might be wise before you start serving one-dish soup meals to learn the language of soup.

First, there's broth, which is a thin soup of meat or shellfish liquid, sometimes with cereals added.

Clear soups, made from meat stock, include consommé (beef, veal, or fowl) and bouillon (beef). A clear soup with strips of vegetables added is a *julienne* soup.

Thick soups include vegetable soups made with stock and vegetables (as in pot-au-feu), or cream soups made with milk and flour, or chowders, where fish and vegetables are cooked in milk or sometimes in water.

A puree differs from a cream soup in that it is thickened by reducing some or all of the ingredients to a pulp. A bisque is a cream soup made of fish, game, or vegetables.

Gumbo is either meat or vegetable soup thickened with okra (remember, we told you filé wasn't easy to come by).

Stock, the basis of many soups, is made by simmering lean meat, fish, fowl, or vegetables in water. Fish stock has its own name—court bouillon. Stock is either white or brown. For white, chicken, turkey, or veal is used; for brown, beef and beef bones or beef and veal go into the pot.

Then there are jellied soups, made from stock or strained vegetable juices thickened with gelatin. Hot-weather favorites, they have a cool clear glamour all their own.

Also in a class by themselves are those Continental specialties, fruit soups. In Denmark, iced fruit soups are laced with claret; the Norwegians produce a soup flavored with sherry and so thick with cherries that eating it is like spooning up a fruit punch. The French are partial to cherry soups; the Hungarians favor peach and apricot soups.

So long as there are canned and frozen soups on the market, preparing a main-dish soup should present no problems. Grandma may have had to keep her soup pot simmering away on the stove for hours; all you have to do is wield a can opener.

If you serve soup frequently one challenge you'll have to face sooner or later is learning how to thicken a soup. There are several ways. Some soups may be thickened with eggs and cream; others by a process of rubbing the ingredients through a sieve or pureeing them in a blender. Many are thickened by adding a "roux," which is a mixture of butter and flour cooked together. The trick, however, is always to add the soup to the roux, not vice versa. In order to avoid curdling when adding eggs or cream to soups, remove the pan from the heat, then add either eggs or cream. Never let the soup boil once you've put it back on the burner. Reheat it with great care, stirring all the while.

Another must is to let your soup simmer gently for ten to fifteen minutes before serving to bring out its full flavor. You'll find, too, that many soups taste even better when reheated a day later. Soups freeze well, although if the recipe calls for cream or milk, don't add it until you plan to serve. Also omit potatoes from a soup you intend to freeze. When it's time for serving, thaw slowly at room temperature or place the pan (covered, of course) in hot running water. Cook soup slowly; don't try to boil soup in a hurry. Extremes, you see, are bad for everyone and everything—even a pot of soup.

Some cooks like to lace soup with wine, but a word of caution here: use the sweet or fruity rather than the dry wines and don't experiment with inexpensive cooking sherry or wine left over from last night's dinner party. Penury of this sort can turn your soup into a disaster. If you're intent on spiking the soup, Madeira, Marsala, or a sweet sherry are the best choices.

Legend has it that the early Romans topped their lentil soup with parsley. From that time on, cooks have been tossing decorations into soup bowls.

The most popular soup decorations are probably croutons. You can economize by making them rather than using the packaged variety. Start with slices of bread—rather than bits of toasted bread. Toast will swell and disintegrate in the soup and make an unattractive soggy mess. Cut the bread into finger lengths, then cube. You may either fry the cubes quickly until crisp in a small amount of hot melted butter or place them (after lightly tossing in melted butter) on an ungreased baking dish and broil under a flame. Stored in a covered tin in a cool, dry place, they'll keep for at least two weeks.

Other accessories for soups include: chopped watercress with white cream soups; curry powder for pea soups; chili powder for corn soups; thin rounds of frankfurters for lentil or pea soups; savory, an herb of the mint family, for bean and fish soups. For fish soups, too, try basil, dill, or fennel. Almonds become chicken soup and sour cream floats beautifully on Borsch. Basil is a friend to tomato soups and nutmeg enhances spinach soup. We could go on—but why not experiment for yourself.

One of the nicest things you can do for any main-dish soup is to serve it in a spectacular way: for example, a chilled jellied madrilene in bright green majolica bowls that look like little heads of lettuce; a hearty New England Clam Chowder in an old-fashioned blue and white enameled dishpan with ladle to match; a hot ham-and-pea soup in a covered ironstone tureen. The traditional rule has been to serve clear soups in two-handled cups and thick soups in bowls, but the only prescription today is to serve your soup from the most interesting container you have.

Some of the following soup recipes are intended for small servings; you may have to increase the ingredients if you are planning to serve them as one-dish meals. Keep in mind that generally, two and a half quarts of soup will provide six main-dish servings.

Black Bean Soup

2 cups dried black beans (1 pound)
1 (2-pound size) shin of beef, with bone
2 beef-bouillon cubes
½ cup sliced onion
1 cup sliced carrot
1½ cups sliced celery, with tops
3 whole cloves
1 bay leaf
1 tablespoon salt
¼ teaspoon pepper
½ cup dry sherry

2 hard-cooked eggs, sliced
1 lemon, thinly sliced
Chopped parsley

1. Soak beans overnight in water to cover.
2. Next day, drain beans. In 8-quart kettle, combine beans, beef, and 8 cups water; bring to boiling. Skim foam from surface.
3. Add bouillon cubes, onion, carrot, celery, cloves, bay leaf, salt, and pepper; return to boiling. Reduce heat; simmer, covered, 3½ hours, or until vegetables and meat are very tender. Remove from heat.
4. Remove the meat from the soup, and cool. Cut meat from the bone, and use for sandwiches another time, if desired.
5. Press the soup mixture through a coarse sieve or food mill, to make a puree.
6. Return to kettle. Add sherry; reheat gently.
7. Serve hot, with slices of hard-cooked egg and lemon over top. Sprinkle with parsley.
Makes 12 cups; 10 to 12 servings.

Boiled-Beef-and-Cabbage Soup

2½ pounds short ribs of beef
1 can (15½ ounces) spaghetti sauce with mushrooms
1 tablespoon thick steak sauce
1½ teaspoons salt
1 medium-size onion, chopped
1 small cabbage, cut in pieces
6 tablespoons lemon juice
1 tablespoon light-brown sugar

1. Wipe short ribs with damp paper towels. Remove any excess fat; cut short ribs into 2-inch pieces.

2. In an 8-quart kettle, combine short ribs with spaghetti sauce, steak sauce, salt, onion, cabbage, and 6 cups water; bring to boiling. Reduce heat, and simmer, covered, for 1¾ hours.

3. Stir in lemon juice and sugar; simmer 15 minutes longer.
Makes about 3½ quarts; 6 to 8 servings.

Borsch

4 large beef marrowbones
1 tablespoon salt
1 (3-pound size) brisket of beef
1 can (1 pound) tomatoes, undrained
1 medium-size onion, peeled and quartered
½ cup chopped celery
4 sprigs parsley
4 whole black peppercorns
1 bay leaf
3 cups coarsely shredded cabbage (1 pound)

1½ cups thickly sliced pared carrot
1 cup chopped onion
2 tablespoons snipped fresh dill
¼ cup cider vinegar
2 tablespoons sugar
1 can (1 pound) julienne beets, undrained

Dairy sour cream

Dark rye bread

1. Place marrowbones, salt, and 2 quarts water in an 8-quart kettle. Cover, and bring to boiling; skim surface. Reduce heat, and simmer, covered, 1 hour.

2. Wipe brisket with damp paper towels. Add beef, tomatoes, quartered onion, celery, parsley, peppercorns, and bay leaf. Simmer, covered, 2 hours longer, or just until meat is tender. Remove from heat.

3. Remove meat and bones; discard bones.

4. Strain soup; return to kettle. You should have about 9 cups liquid. Refrigerate soup, covered, several hours.

5. Skim off fat. Add cabbage, carrot, chopped onion, dill, vinegar, and sugar; bring to boiling. Reduce heat; simmer, covered, 40 minutes, or until vegetables are tender.

6. Add beets; cook 10 minutes longer.

7. To serve: Slice brisket of beef, and put several slices in individual soup bowls. Pour soup over meat. Top with spoonfuls of sour cream. If

desired, garnish with snipped dill. Serve with dark rye bread. Meat can
be served separately, if desired.

Makes 3 quarts; 8 servings.

Frankfurter-Cabbage Soup

½ pound frankfurters or knockwurst	2 cups finely chopped cabbage
¼ cup finely chopped onion	2 teaspoons salt
½ cup diced celery	¼ teaspoon pepper
1 cup diced pared raw potato	2 teaspoons brown sugar
1 can (13¾ ounces) chicken broth undiluted	1 teaspoon caraway seed, tied in cheesecloth bag
3 cups milk	1 cup light cream

1. Cut frankfurters into ¼-inch slices or knockwurst into chunks.

2. In 4-quart kettle, combine frankfurters, onion, celery, potato, and
chicken broth; bring to boiling. Reduce heat; simmer, covered, 15
minutes.

3. Add milk, cabbage, salt, pepper, brown sugar, and caraway seed;
bring back to boiling. Reduce heat; simmer, covered, 25 minutes longer.

4. Discard caraway seed. Stir in light cream. Serve hot.

Makes about 2 quarts; 6 to 8 servings.

Hearty Highland Soup

Meatballs

1½ pounds coarsely ground lamb	¾ cup sliced celery, ¼ inch thick
⅓ cup grated Parmesan cheese	¼ cup chopped onion
1 egg, slightly beaten	1 clove garlic, crushed
3 tablespoons milk	¾ teaspoon bouquet garni
1 tablespoon chopped parsley	1 teaspoon salt
¼ teaspoon dried crushed rosemary	3¾ cups boiling water
1 teaspoon salt	3 cans (10¾-ounce size) condensed Scotch broth, undiluted
2 tablespoons salad oil	
1¼ cups diagonally sliced pared carrots, ¼ inch thick	

1. Make Meatballs: In large bowl, lightly toss lamb with cheese, egg, milk, parsley, rosemary, and salt just until combined. Gently shape the mixture into balls 1½ inches in diameter.

2. Heat salad oil in large skillet. Add meatballs; sauté, over medium heat, turning, until nicely browned all over—about 20 minutes in all.

3. Remove meatballs as they brown; drain.

4. Meanwhile, in a 6-quart kettle, combine carrots, celery, onion, garlic, bouquet garni, salt, and boiling water. Bring to boiling; reduce heat, and cook, covered, 20 minutes.

5. To cooked vegetables, add soup, mixing well. Add meatballs; continue cooking, covered, 30 minutes longer.

Makes about 2 quarts; 6 to 8 servings.

Hamburger-Vegetable Soup

Meatballs

1½ pounds ground beef chuck
1 egg, slightly beaten
½ cup soft bread crumbs (1 slice)
¼ teaspoon salt
1 tablespoon chopped parsley

2 tablespoons butter or margarine
1 can (10½ ounces) condensed beef broth, undiluted
1 can (1 pound, 12 ounces) tomatoes, undrained

1 envelope (1³⁸ ounces) dry onion soup mix
2 cups sliced pared carrots (4 or 5 medium-size)
¼ cup chopped celery tops
¼ cup chopped parsley
¼ teaspoon pepper
¼ teaspoon dried oregano leaves
¼ teaspoon dried basil leaves
1 bay leaf

Chopped parsley (optional)

1. Make Meatballs: In medium-size bowl, combine beef, egg, 3 tablespoons water, the bread crumbs, salt, and parsley; mix lightly. With hands, lightly shape into 24 balls.

2. In hot butter in a 4½-quart kettle, sauté meatballs, a single layer at a time, until browned on all sides. Drain off fat. Set the meatballs aside.

3. In same kettle, combine 2 cups water, the beef broth, tomatoes, onion soup mix, carrots, celery tops, parsley, pepper, oregano, basil,

and bay leaf; bring to boiling. Reduce heat, and simmer, covered and stirring occasionally to break up tomatoes, 30 minutes. Add meatballs; simmer 20 minutes longer.

4. Serve in tureen or individual bowls. Garnish with chopped parsley, if desired.

Makes about 2 quarts; 6 servings.

Leek Soup

1 (1½-pound size) piece of bacon	4 leeks, washed
1 pound potatoes (3 medium-size)	½ small head cabbage
	1½ teaspoons salt
½ pound carrots (4 medium-size)	⅛ teaspoon pepper
	1 tablespoon chopped parsley

1. In 6-quart saucepan or kettle, bring the bacon, in 2 quarts water, to boiling. Cover; simmer 1½ hours. Cool; refrigerate overnight.

2. Next day, pare potatoes; cut into ½-inch cubes. Pare carrots; slice thinly. Trim root ends and green tops of leeks, leaving leeks 7 inches long; discard trimmings. Cut leeks into ¼-inch slices. Shred cabbage finely, to make 3 cups.

3. Remove fat from refrigerated broth. Bring broth, with bacon, to boiling. Add potato, carrot, salt, and pepper; simmer, covered, 40 minutes.

4. Lift out bacon; keep warm.

5. Add leek and cabbage to broth; simmer, covered, 10 minutes longer, or until vegetables are tender.

6. To serve: Cut bacon into ½-inch cubes; return to broth. Ladle broth, bacon, and vegetables into soup tureen. Sprinkle with parsley.

Makes about 2½ quarts; 8 to 10 servings.

Corned-Beef-Hash and Leek Soup

1 can (15½ ounces) corned-beef hash	⅛ teaspoon pepper
	Dash salt
1 packet (1⅞ ounces) dehydrated cream of leek soup mix	¼ teaspoon dried rosemary leaves, crushed
	⅓ cup light cream
1 cup milk	

1. Drain corned-beef hash, removing any excess fat.
2. In medium-size saucepan, combine soup mix with water as package label directs.
3. Add milk and hash, breaking hash with fork. Bring to boiling; reduce heat, and simmer, uncovered, 2 minutes.
4. Add pepper, salt, rosemary, and cream; heat, stirring, until the soup is hot.
Makes about 1½ quarts; 4 to 6 servings.

Lentil Soup with Ham

1 (2-pound size) fully cooked ham shank
1½ cups dried lentils
3 tablespoons butter or margarine
½ cup chopped celery
½ cup chopped leek
½ cup chopped onion
1 small clove garlic, crushed

1¾ teaspoons salt
¼ teaspoon dried thyme leaves
¼ teaspoon coarsely ground black pepper
1 cup sliced frankfurters (about 3)

Dairy sour cream
Chopped parsley

1. Trim excess fat from ham shank.
2. In large kettle, combine ham shank and lentils with 5 cups cold water; bring to boiling.
3. Reduce heat; simmer, covered, 1 hour.
4. Meanwhile, melt butter in medium-size skillet. Add celery, leek, onion, and garlic; sauté 5 minutes.
5. Add sautéed vegetables, salt, thyme, pepper, and 2 cups water to ham shank and lentils. Simmer, covered, until lentils are tender—about 30 minutes.
6. Remove ham from soup; cool. Then cut meat from bone, and dice.
7. With potato masher, mash vegetables, right in kettle; leave some lentils whole.
8. Add diced ham to soup, along with frankfurters; simmer, covered, 30 minutes longer. (For a very thick soup, simmer uncovered.)
9. Serve topped with sour cream and parsley.
Makes 8 cups; 8 servings.

Petite Marmite

1 (4-pound size) shin of beef
2 pounds chicken wings and
   necks
2 cans (10½-ounce size)
   condensed chicken broth,
   undiluted
2½ tablespoons salt
12 whole black peppercorns
3 sprigs parsley
¾ teaspoon dried thyme leaves
¾ teaspoon dried marjoram
   leaves
1 bay leaf
2 cups sliced pared carrot (¼
   inch thick)

2 cups sliced leek (¼ inch
   thick)
1 cup sliced celery (¼ inch
   thick)
3 white turnips, peeled and
   quartered (1 pound)
1 large onion, sliced
4 cups shredded cabbage (1¼
   pounds)

French bread, sliced 1 inch thick
Grated Parmesan cheese

1. Rinse beef and chicken parts in cold water.

2. Place beef, chicken, and chicken broth in 6-quart kettle. Add 2½ quarts water; cover the kettle, and slowly bring the mixture to a boil; skim surface.

3. Add salt, black peppercorns, parsley sprigs, thyme, marjoram, and bay leaf. Cover kettle again, and simmer 2½ hours, or just until the meat is tender.

4. Remove meat from soup; set aside.

5. Strain soup through coarse strainer. Pour back into kettle. Discard chicken pieces and the seasonings.

6. Add carrot, leek, celery, turnip, and onion. Simmer, covered, 1½ hours. Meanwhile, cut beef into large cubes; set aside.

7. Add cabbage; cook, covered, 10 minutes, or just until cabbage is tender. Skim off excess fat.

8. Sprinkle one side of each bread slice with cheese. Brown under broiler 1 minute, or until the cheese is bubbly.

9. To serve: Pour soup into individual hot bowls. Add a few pieces of meat to each serving. Top with toasted bread slices; serve immediately.

Makes about 3½ quarts; 10 servings.

Oxtail Soup

3 pounds oxtails, cut up
3 tablespoons butter or margarine
1 can (10½ ounces) condensed beef consommé, undiluted
2 teaspoons salt
2 teaspoons Worcestershire sauce
1 teaspoon dried thyme leaves
1 teaspoon dried tarragon leaves
6 whole black peppercorns
1 bay leaf

1 clove garlic, crushed
1 egg white
1 eggshell
2 cups diced white turnip (¾ pound)
1½ cups diced pared carrot (4 medium-size)
1½ cups sliced celery
1 cup chopped onion
½ cup claret

Chopped parsley

1. Wipe oxtails with damp paper towels.

2. In hot butter in deep, 6-quart kettle, slowly brown oxtails on all sides—about 30 minutes.

3. Add 2 quarts water, the consommé, salt, Worcestershire, thyme, tarragon, black peppercorns, bay leaf, and garlic; bring to boiling. Reduce heat, and simmer, covered, 3½ hours. Remove from heat.

4. Remove oxtails with slotted spoon, and remove their excess fat. If desired, take meat off bones. Refrigerate, covered.

5. Strain broth. Refrigerate, covered, until chilled—several hours or overnight.

6. About 2 hours before serving, skim fat from broth. Slightly beat egg white with 2 tablespoons water. Add with crushed eggshell to cold stock in large saucepan. Bring to boiling, stirring constantly; boil 2 minutes. Remove from heat; add 1 cup cold water; let broth stand 30 minutes. Then strain into a large kettle.

7. Add oxtails or oxtail meat, turnip, carrot, celery, and onion; bring to boiling. Reduce heat, and simmer, covered, 30 minutes, or until vegetables are just tender.

8. Add claret; simmer 15 minutes longer. Pour into soup tureen or individual bowls. Garnish with parsley.

Makes about 2½ quarts; 8 servings.

Hearty Pea Soup

1 pound quick-cooking split green peas (2 cups)
⅛ pound salt pork or bacon, coarsely chopped (about ⅓ cup)
½ cup coarsely chopped leek or green onion
1½ cups coarsely chopped celery
1 cup coarsely chopped onion

2 (1-pound size) pig's knuckles
2 parsley sprigs
1 bay leaf
⅛ teaspoon dried rosemary leaves
Salt

1 tablespoon chopped parsley

1. In a 6-quart kettle, combine peas and 3 quarts water. Bring to boiling; reduce heat, and simmer, covered, 45 minutes.

2. Meanwhile, in small skillet, sauté pork several minutes. Add leek, celery, and onion; sauté, stirring, until onion is golden—about 5 minutes.

3. Wipe pig's knuckles with damp paper towels. Add to kettle along with pork and sautéed vegetables, parsley sprigs, bay leaf, rosemary, and 2 teaspoons salt. Bring back to boiling; reduce heat, and simmer, covered, 2 hours, or until pig's knuckles are tender and meat begins to fall off bones. Remove from heat.

4. With slotted utensil, lift out pig's knuckles to cool. Remove meat from bones; discard skin, fat, and bones.

5. If necessary, skim fat from soup. Put soup with vegetables through coarse sieve, pureeing vegetables.

6. Pour back into kettle. Add meat from pig's knuckles; reheat slowly, stirring occasionally, until heated through. Add salt to taste; heat 5 minutes longer.

7. Sprinkle with chopped parsley.

Makes about 3 quarts; 10 servings.

Sauerkraut-Beef Soup

5 pounds beef bones (marrowbone and knucklebone
3 pounds boneless shin beef

2 cups coarsely chopped onion
2 cups coarsely chopped pared carrot
3 cloves garlic

1½ teaspoons dried thyme leaves
2 large bay leaves
1 can (1 pound, 12 ounces) tomatoes, undrained
12 cups thinly sliced cabbage (3 pounds)
4 beef-bouillon cubes
1 tablespoon salt

1 teaspoon cracked black pepper
½ cup lemon juice
¼ cup sugar (optional)
1 can (1 pound, 11 ounces) sauerkraut, drained

Dairy sour cream

1. Preheat oven to 450° F.

2. Place beef bones, shin beef, onion, carrot, garlic, thyme, and bay leaves in a large, shallow roasting pan. Bake 15 minutes; stir with large spoon, and bake 15 minutes longer, or until meat is brown.

3. Transfer mixture to a 10- to 12-quart kettle. Add 3½ quarts water, the tomatoes, cabbage, bouillon cubes, salt, and pepper. Bring to boiling; skim off fat and foam.

4. Reduce heat, and simmer, covered, 2 hours, or until meat is tender. Remove bones and meat from soup. Discard bones. Cut meat into 1-inch cubes; return to soup.

5. Add lemon juice, sugar, and sauerkraut. Bring to boiling; reduce heat; simmer, covered, 1 hour longer. Skim off fat.

6. Serve hot, in large soup bowls. Pass the sour cream.

Makes 6½ quarts; about 16 servings.

Vegetable-Barley Soup

3 pounds beef short ribs
2 cans (1-pound, 12-ounce size) tomatoes, undrained
1 tablespoon salt
2 bay leaves
1 package (10 ounces) frozen cut green beans

1 can (12 ounces) whole-kernel corn, undrained
1 cup chopped onion
½ cup barley
½ teaspoon dried oregano leaves
½ teaspoon dried basil leaves
1 clove garlic, crushed

1. Place short ribs, tomatoes, salt, and bay leaves in 8-quart kettle; add 1 quart water. Cover, and bring to boiling. Skim surface.

2. Reduce heat; simmer, covered, 2 hours.

3. Add beans, corn, onion, barley, oregano, basil, and garlic. Simmer, covered, 1 hour longer, or until tender.

4. Remove meat and bones; discard bones.

5. Cool meat. Cut into slices; add to soup. Refrigerate several hours.

6. Just before serving, skim fat from surface. Slowly heat soup to boiling.

Makes 3 quarts; 10 servings.

Vegetable-Beef Soup

1 (4-pound size) shin beef, with bone
2 tablespoons salt
2 cups thinly sliced cabbage (½ pound)
1½ cups chopped onion
½ pound carrots, pared and cut in 1-inch pieces
¾ cup chopped celery
¼ cup chopped green pepper
1 can (1 pound, 12 ounces) tomatoes, undrained (3½ cups)

1 package (9 ounces) frozen cut green beans
1 can (12 ounces) whole-kernel corn, drained
1 pared raw potato, cubed (1 cup)
2 tablespoons chopped parsley
1 can (6 ounces) tomato paste
¼ teaspoon cloves
1 teaspoon sugar
½ teaspoon pepper
½ cup barley

1. Place beef, 1 tablespoon salt, and 4 quarts water in very large kettle. Cover; bring to boiling. Skim surface.

2. Add cabbage, onion, carrot, celery, green pepper, and tomatoes. Bring to boiling; simmer, covered, 30 minutes.

3. Add 1 tablespoon salt and the rest of ingredients, except barley; simmer, covered, 2 hours. Add barley; simmer 1 hour longer.

4. Remove meat from kettle; let meat cool.

5. Remove meat from bone. Cut into cubes; add to soup. Refrigerate overnight.

6. Skim fat from surface. Bring to boiling. Reduce heat; simmer, uncovered, 30 minutes.

Makes 6½ quarts; about 16 servings.

Manhattan Clam Chowder

4 slices bacon, diced	2 teaspoons salt
1 cup sliced onion	¼ teaspoon black pepper
1 cup diced celery	1 bay leaf
½ cup diced green pepper	1½ teaspoons dried thyme leaves
1 can (1 pound, 12 ounces) tomatoes, undrained	3 cups diced potato
	2 tablespoons chopped parsley
1 can (7½ ounces) minced clams	

1. In 6-quart Dutch oven or kettle, sauté diced bacon until it is almost crisp.

2. Add onion, celery, and green pepper; cook vegetables, over low heat and stirring occasionally, 5 minutes.

3. Add tomatoes to vegetables in kettle.

4. Drain clams, reserving liquid; set clams aside. Add water to clam liquid to make 1 quart. Pour into kettle. Add salt, pepper, bay leaf, and thyme. Bring to boiling; reduce heat; simmer chowder, covered, 45 minutes.

5. Add potato; cover, and cook 20 minutes.

6. Add reserved clams; simmer, uncovered, 15 minutes. Add chopped parsley. Serve hot.

Makes 3 quarts; 10 servings.

New England Clam Chowder

2 slices bacon	1 pint shucked fresh clams, or 2 cans (10½-ounce size) minced clams
1 cup finely chopped onion	
2 cups cubed pared potato	
1 teaspoon salt	2 cups half-and-half
Dash pepper	2 tablespoons butter or margarine

1. Chop bacon coarsely. Sauté in large kettle until almost crisp. Add onion; cook about 5 minutes.

2. Add cubed potato, salt, pepper, and 1 cup water. Cook, uncovered, 15 minutes, or until potato is fork-tender.

3. Meanwhile, drain clams, reserving clam liquid. Chop clams coarsely.

4. Add clams, ½ cup clam liquid, the half-and-half, and butter to kettle; mix well. Heat about 3 minutes; do not boil.

Makes about 1½ quarts; 4 servings.

New England Fish Chowder

2 pounds halibut fillets	2 cups boiling water
8 slices bacon, cut in ½-inch pieces	3 cups milk
1½ cups chopped onion	1 cup light cream
3 cups diced (¼-inch) pared potato	⅛ teaspoon pepper
3 teaspoons salt	Dash cayenne
	Crackers

1. Rinse halibut fillets under cold water; drain. Cut in ½-inch pieces.

2. In 6-quart Dutch oven or kettle, sauté bacon until almost crisp. Pour off bacon fat; return 2 tablespoons fat to Dutch oven; discard the rest.

3. Add onion, and sauté until golden—about 5 minutes.

4. Add potato, 1 teaspoon salt, and the boiling water. Bring to boiling; reduce heat; simmer, covered, 10 minutes. Add fish; simmer, covered, 10 minutes longer.

5. Heat milk and cream to lukewarm.

6. Add milk mixture, remaining salt, the pepper, and cayenne to chowder. Heat over low heat just until bubbles appear around edge of pan. Do not let boil.

7. Ladle into bowls. Float crackers on each serving.

Makes about 4 quarts; 12 servings.

Scallop Chowder

6 slices bacon, diced	1 tablespoon chopped parsley
1 cup sliced onion	1 can (1 pound, 12 ounces) tomatoes, undrained
1 cup green pepper strips	
1 cup thin carrot strips	1 bottle (7½ ounces) clam juice

2 teaspoons salt
1 bay leaf
1½ teaspoons bottled steak sauce
¾ teaspoon dried thyme leaves

3 medium-size potatoes (about 1 pound), pared and diced
1½ pounds sea scallops, washed and drained

1. In 6-quart kettle, sauté bacon until almost crisp. Add onion, green pepper, carrot, and parsley; cook, over low heat and stirring occasionally, until onion is tender—about 10 minutes.

2. Add tomatoes, clam juice, salt, bay leaf, steak sauce, thyme, and 1½ cups water; bring to boiling. Reduce heat; simmer, covered, 35 minutes.

3. Add potatoes; cover; simmer 30 minutes.

4. Add scallops; simmer, uncovered, 15 minutes.

Makes about 2½ quarts; 6 main-dish servings.

Bacon-and-Bean Chowder

½ pound sliced bacon, cut crosswise into ½-inch pieces
½ cup chopped onion
½ cup chopped green pepper
¾ cup chopped celery, with tops
2 tablespoons flour
2 cans (1-pound size) red kidney beans, undrained

½ cup thinly sliced pared carrot
¼ cup chopped parsley
1 bay leaf
¼ teaspoon salt
⅛ teaspoon pepper
¼ teaspoon dried thyme leaves
3 beef-bouillon cubes

1. In large saucepan, over low heat, sauté bacon until crisp. Drain, reserving ¼ cup drippings.

2. In reserved drippings, sauté onion, green pepper, and celery about 5 minutes, or until tender.

3. Remove from heat. Stir in flour. Add kidney beans, carrot slices, parsley, bay leaf, salt, pepper, thyme leaves, bouillon cubes, and 3 cups water.

4. Slowly bring to boiling, stirring occasionally. Reduce heat; simmer, covered, about 40 minutes, stirring several times.

5. Sprinkle bacon over top of chowder; heat several minutes longer. Serve at once.

Makes 2 quarts; 6 to 8 servings.

Frankfurter Chowder

3 tablespoons butter or
   margarine
2 small onions, sliced
1 clove garlic, crushed
4 frankfurters
½ small cabbage, coarsely
   shredded (4 cups)
2 medium-size potatoes, pared
   and cubed (2 cups)
3 large carrots, pared and diced

2 stalks celery, sliced in ¼-inch
   pieces
2 cans (10½-ounce size)
   condensed beef broth,
   undiluted
2 teaspoons salt
⅛ teaspoon pepper

2 tablespoons chopped parsley

1. In hot butter in 6-quart kettle, sauté onion and garlic until tender but not brown.

2. Cut frankfurters in half crosswise; then quarter each half lengthwise. Add to kettle with cabbage, potato, carrot, celery, beef broth, salt, pepper, and 4 cups water.

3. Bring to boiling. Reduce heat, and simmer, covered, 30 to 40 minutes, or until potato is tender.

4. Turn into heated tureen. Garnish with chopped parsley.

Makes about 2 quarts; 6 to 8 servings.

Note: This soup may be made a day ahead, then reheated.

Creamy Corn Chowder

2 slices bacon, diced
1 small onion, thinly sliced
2 medium-size potatoes, pared
   and diced (2 cups)
1 can (1 pound) cream-style
   corn
1½ cups milk

2 tablespoons butter or
   margarine
1¼ teaspoons salt
½ teaspoon sugar
⅛ teaspoon pepper

Chopped parsley

1. In medium-size saucepan, sauté bacon and onion until onion is golden.

2. Add potatoes and ¾ cup water; bring to boiling. Boil gently, covered, about 10 minutes, or until potatoes are tender but not mushy.

3. Add corn, milk, butter, salt, sugar, and pepper; simmer, covered, 5 minutes, or until hot.

4. Serve in soup bowls. Garnish with parsley.

Makes about 2 quarts; 6 to 8 servings.

Clam-and-Corn Chowder

2   bacon slices, diced
½   cup chopped onion
2   medium-size potatoes, pared
    and cubed
1½ teaspoons salt
1   teaspoon celery salt
⅛   teaspoon pepper
2   cans (7½-ounce size) minced
    clams, undrained

1   can (8¾ ounces) cream-style
    corn
2   cups milk
2   tablespoons butter or
    margarine
9   soda crackers, crushed (⅔
    cup)

1   tablespoon chopped parsley

1. In 4-quart kettle, sauté bacon until crisp. Add onion; sauté until tender—about 5 minutes.

2. Add potato, salt, celery salt, pepper, and 1½ cups water; cook, covered, 10 minutes.

3. Add clams, corn, milk, and butter; cook, covered, 3 minutes longer, or until potato is tender.

4. Sprinkle in crackers; heat slightly. Serve hot, sprinkled with parsley.

Makes about 1½ quarts; 4 to 6 servings.

Chicken-and-Corn Chowder

1   (3-pound size) ready-to-cook
    whole roasting chicken
2   tablespoons butter or
    margarine
2   cans (10½-ounce size)
    condensed chicken broth,
    undiluted
1   large onion, peeled and
    quartered
1   stalk celery with leaves, cut
    up

1½ teaspoons salt
¼   teaspoon pepper
¼   teaspoon saffron
2   cups (4 ounces) medium-size
    noodles
1   package (10 ounces) frozen
    whole-kernel corn
2   hard-cooked eggs, coarsely
    chopped
2   tablespoons chopped parsley

1. Rinse chicken well in cold water. Dry with paper towels. Brown lightly in the butter in a deep, 8-quart kettle. Add 1½ quarts water, the chicken broth, onion, celery, salt, pepper, and saffron.

2. Bring to boiling. Reduce heat, and simmer, covered, 1 hour, or until chicken is tender.

3. Lift out chicken; set aside. Strain broth. If necessary, skim fat from broth. Add water, if necessary, to make 8 cups.

4. Add noodles and corn to broth; bring to boiling. Reduce heat, and boil gently, uncovered, 20 minutes.

5. Return chicken to kettle, and simmer until heated through.

6. Add chopped egg, parsley, and, if necessary, a little more salt and pepper. Turn into soup tureen.

7. When serving, lift chicken out of soup. Cut it into pieces, and divide among soup bowls. Fill bowls with soup mixture.

Makes about 2½ quarts; 8 servings.

Potato-Cheese Chowder

1½ cups diced pared potatoes	Dash pepper
2 chicken-bouillon cubes	2 cups milk
2 tablespoons butter or margarine	1½ cups grated sharp Cheddar cheese
¼ cup diced green pepper	
2 tablespoons flour	
1 teaspoon salt	Finely chopped parsley

1. In medium-size saucepan, combine potatoes and 2 cups water; bring to boiling. Reduce heat, and simmer 15 minutes, or until potatoes are tender.

2. Drain potatoes, reserving 1½ cups liquid. Add bouillon cubes to liquid; stir to dissolve.

3. Melt butter in same saucepan. Add green pepper, and sauté until tender—about 5 minutes.

4. Remove from heat. Stir in flour, salt, and pepper. Gradually stir in potato liquid and milk.

5. Bring the mixture to boiling; reduce heat, and simmer 2 minutes.

6. Remove from heat. Add cheese and potatoes, stirring until cheese is melted.

7. Serve topped with parsley.

Makes about 5 cups; 4 to 6 servings.

Turkey Chowder

3 cups turkey stock
1 cup pared diced potato
2 teaspoons minced onion
½ to 1 teaspoon salt
Dash pepper

1 can (10½ ounces) condensed cream of celery soup, undiluted
¼ cup crumbled cooked bacon
2 tablespoons chopped parsley
½ cup diced turkey

1. In 3½-quart saucepan, combine turkey stock with potato, onion, salt, and pepper; bring to boiling. Reduce heat; simmer, covered, about 20 minutes, or until potatoes are tender.

2. Remove from heat. Add cream of celery soup; mix well. Add remaining ingredients; reheat gently.

Makes about 5 cups; 5 to 6 servings.

American Bouillabaisse

¼ cup olive or salad oil
3 tablespoons butter or margarine
1 clove garlic, crushed
2 cups sliced onion
1 cup green-pepper strips
½ cup sliced celery
2 leeks, chopped
1 tablespoon salt
¼ teaspoon pepper
1½ teaspoons dried thyme leaves
⅛ teaspoon crumbled saffron
1 bay leaf
1 can (1 pound) tomatoes, undrained

1 can (10½ ounces) tomato puree
1 cup dry white wine
2 pounds haddock fillets, cut into serving pieces
1 pound codfish fillets, cut into serving pieces
1 can (7½ ounces) king-crab meat, drained
1 can (4½ ounces) deveined shrimp, drained

2 tablespoons chopped parsley

1. Slowly heat oil and butter in large saucepan. Add garlic, onion, green pepper, celery, and leeks; sauté, stirring, about 5 minutes.

2. Add salt, pepper, thyme, saffron, bay leaf, tomatoes, tomato puree, wine, haddock, and cod; bring to boiling. Reduce heat; simmer, covered, 15 minutes.

3. Meanwhile, separate crab meat, removing any cartilage. Rinse shrimp in cold water; drain.

4. Add crab meat and shrimp to bouillabaisse; simmer, covered, 15 minutes longer. (If mixture seems too thick, stir in a little boiling water.)

5. Serve sprinkled with parsley.

Makes about 2 quarts; 6 to 8 servings.

Shrimp Gumbo

4 tablespoons butter or margarine	1 package (10 ounces) frozen whole okra, slightly thawed
1 tablespoon flour	½ cup chopped onion
1 pound raw shrimp, shelled and deveined	2 tablespoons chopped green pepper
2 teaspoons crab or shrimp boil, tied in a cheesecloth bag (see p. 195)	1 can (8 ounces) tomato sauce
	1 can (8 ounces) tomatoes
1 teaspoon salt	
Dash pepper	2 to 3 cups cooked white rice
	Chopped parsley

1. In large saucepan or Dutch oven, melt 2 tablespoons butter. Remove from heat; blend in flour until smooth. Return to heat; add shrimp; cook, stirring often, 3 to 4 minutes.

2. Add 2 cups water, the crab or shrimp boil, salt, and pepper. Bring to boiling; reduce heat; simmer, covered, 15 minutes.

3. Meanwhile, cut okra in 1-inch pieces. Heat remaining butter in medium-size saucepan. Sauté okra, onion, and green pepper until tender—about 10 minutes. Stir in tomato sauce and tomatoes.

4. Add tomato mixture to shrimp; simmer 30 minutes longer.

5. Mound ½ cup cooked rice in each large soup plate. Ladle gumbo over rice. Sprinkle with parsley.

Makes about 2 quarts; 4 to 6 servings.

Crab-Meat Bisque

2 cans (7½-ounce size)
   king-crab meat
3 tablespoons butter or
   margarine
¾ cup finely chopped onion
4 cups milk
2 cups light cream

2 teaspoons salt
Dash pepper
¾ cup sherry
⅓ cup unsifted all-purpose flour

Chopped parsley

1. Drain crab meat; reserve liquid. Remove any cartilage from crab meat.

2. Melt butter in a 3-quart saucepan. Add onion, crab meat, and reserved liquid; simmer 5 minutes.

3. Meanwhile, heat milk with cream until bubbles form around edge of pan.

4. Stir into crab mixture along with salt and pepper.

5. In small bowl, combine ½ cup sherry with the flour, mixing well. Stir into crab mixture.

6. Bring to boiling; reduce heat, and simmer 20 minutes. Stir in remaining ¼ cup sherry. Sprinkle the bisque with parsley before serving.

Makes 2 quarts; about 8 servings.

Lobster Bisque

1 small carrot, sliced
1 medium-size onion, peeled
   and quartered
1 teaspoon salt
2 whole black peppercorns
1 bay leaf
Pinch dried thyme leaves
1 sprig parsley
¾ cup dry white wine

3 (5- to 8-ounce size) frozen
   rock-lobster tails, unthawed
½ cup butter or margarine
3 tablespoons flour
2 cups heavy cream
1 to 2 tablespoons sherry
   (optional)

Paprika

1. In 4-quart saucepan, combine carrot, onion, salt, peppercorns, bay leaf, thyme, parsley, and 6 cups water.

2. Add wine and lobster tails; bring just to boiling. Reduce heat; simmer, covered, 5 minutes.

3. Remove lobster tails from cooking liquid; cool. Continue to cook liquid, uncovered, about 45 minutes, to reduce to about half of original volume. Strain; liquid should measure 2 cups. Reserve.

4. Melt butter in same saucepan. Remove from heat; stir in flour to make a smooth mixture.

5. Gradually add reserved cooking liquid, stirring until smooth. Bring to boiling, stirring; reduce heat; simmer 10 minutes, stirring occasionally.

6. Meanwhile, remove meat from shells; cut into very small pieces.

7. Gradually add cream, then lobster and sherry. Reheat gently—do not boil. Sprinkle with paprika before serving.

Makes 5 cups; 6 servings.

Oyster Bisque

2 cans (10¼-ounce size) frozen condensed oyster stew, undiluted
3 cups milk
2½ teaspoons instant minced onion
2 tablespoons dried celery flakes
2 bay leaves
¼ teaspoon garlic powder
⅛ teaspoon mace
Dash pepper
½ cup sherry
4 tablespoons chopped parsley

1. Partially thaw oyster stew according to label directions.

2. In medium-size saucepan, combine all ingredients, except sherry and parsley, with ¾ cup water; stir until well mixed.

3. Over high heat, bring to boiling, uncovered; stir occasionally.

4. Reduce heat; simmer 10 minutes, stirring occasionally.

5. Remove from heat. Stir in sherry and parsley. Serve at once, in mugs.

Makes about 2 quarts; 6 servings.

Mushroom Bisque

2 packages (2-ounce size) dried cream of mushroom soup mix
2 cans (10½-ounce size) chicken consommé
¾ cup milk
½ teaspoon nutmeg
Dash cayenne
⅛ teaspoon dry mustard
½ cup sherry

1. Combine all ingredients except sherry with 2¼ cups water in medium-size saucepan.
2. With wire whisk or rotary beater, beat until well mixed.
3. Over high heat, bring to boiling, uncovered; stir occasionally. Reduce heat; simmer 5 minutes, stirring occasionally.
4. Remove from heat. Stir in sherry. Serve at once, in mugs.
Makes about 1½ quarts; 6 servings.

Cream of Asparagus Soup

2 packages (10-ounce size) frozen cut asparagus spears
½ cup butter or margarine
1 cup finely chopped onion
1 cup finely chopped celery
2 tablespoons finely chopped parsley
¼ cup unsifted all-purpose flour

5 cans (10½-ounce size) chicken broth, undiluted
1½ tablespoons salt
¼ teaspoon white pepper
1½ teaspoons curry powder
½ cup Madeira wine
2 cups heavy cream

Finely chopped parsley

1. Pour boiling water over the frozen asparagus spears to thaw; drain.
2. In hot butter in large skillet, sauté asparagus, onion, celery, and 2 tablespoons parsley 10 minutes, stirring occasionally.
3. Remove from heat. Stir in flour. Gradually stir in 3 cups chicken broth.
4. Blend in blender, at high speed, covered, until smooth.
5. Combine with rest of chicken broth in a large saucepan; bring the mixture to boiling, stirring occasionally.
6. Reduce heat. Stir in salt, pepper, curry powder, Madeira wine, and cream; heat, stirring, until thoroughly hot.
7. Serve garnished with chopped parsley.
Makes 3½ quarts; 10 to 12 servings.

Cream of Lima Bean Soup

2 cups dried lima beans
⅔ cup sliced onion
½ cup finely chopped celery
1 pound ready-to-eat ham, cubed

1½ teaspoons salt
¼ teaspoon pepper
¼ cup chopped parsley
½ cup light cream

1. In medium-size bowl, add cold water to beans to cover. Refrigerate, covered, overnight.

2. Next day, drain beans. In large saucepan, combine beans with onion, celery, ham, 1 teaspoon salt, and 6 cups water; bring to boiling. Reduce heat; simmer, covered, 2 hours.

3. Stir in remaining salt, the pepper, and parsley; simmer 15 minutes longer.

4. Just before serving, stir in cream.

Makes about 2 quarts; 6 to 8 servings.

Cream of Squash Soup

1 **butternut squash* (about 3 pounds)**	¼ **teaspoon salt** **Dash white pepper**
2 **cans (10½-ounce size) condensed chicken broth, undiluted**	1 **cup heavy cream** ¼ **teaspoon ground nutmeg**

1. Preheat oven to 400° F. Bake whole squash about 1 hour, or until tender when pierced with a fork.

2. Let squash cool slightly. Cut in half lengthwise; discard seeds. With a spoon, scoop squash pulp from the skin.

3. In electric blender, combine half of squash pulp and 1 can broth; blend at low speed until well combined, then at high speed until smooth. Turn into bowl. Repeat with remaining squash and broth. Stir in salt and pepper.

4. Refrigerate soup, covered, overnight.

5. At serving time, heat squash mixture just to boiling. Gradually stir in ½ cup cream; cook slowly until heated through. Taste for seasoning, adding more salt and pepper if necessary.

6. Meanwhile, beat remaining cream just until stiff.

7. Serve soup very hot. Garnish each serving with a spoonful of whipped cream; sprinkle with nutmeg.

Makes about 1½ quarts; 6 servings.

---

*Or use 3 packages (12-ounce size) frozen squash, partially thawed.

Chilled Avocado Soup

3 ripe avocados (about 2 pounds)
2 cans (13-ounce size) vichyssoise
2 cups light cream
1 cup chicken broth, undiluted
¼ cup lemon juice
½ avocado, for garnish

1. Peel 3 avocados. Slice 1½ into electric-blender container. Add 1 can vichyssoise, 1 cup cream, ½ cup chicken broth, and 2 tablespoons lemon juice.

2. Blend, at high speed, ½ to 1 minute, or until smooth. Pour into large bowl. Repeat. (Or press through a sieve into a large bowl; beat with electric mixer, at low speed, until smooth.)

3. Refrigerate soup, covered, until very well chilled—at least 4 hours.

4. Serve in a large glass bowl, decorated with avocado slices.

Makes about 2 quarts; 6 to 8 servings.

Chilled Green-Pea Soup

2 packages (10-ounce size) frozen green peas
½ cup finely chopped green onion
½ teaspoon salt
Dash nutmeg
1 can (10½ ounces) condensed chicken broth, undiluted
½ cup heavy cream

Chives (optional)

1. In medium-size saucepan, combine peas, onion, salt, nutmeg, and ¾ cup water. Bring to boiling; reduce heat, and simmer, covered, 15 minutes, or until peas are very tender.

2. Pour peas with liquid into electric blender. Cover, and blend at low speed to mix, then at high speed 1 minute, or until smooth. Stir in chicken broth.

3. Refrigerate, covered, until well chilled—at least 4 hours.

4. To serve: Stir in cream. Pour into chilled bouillon cups. Sprinkle with snipped chives, if desired.

Makes about 1½ quarts; 6 servings.

Chilled Jellied Gazpacho

1 cup boiling water	Few drops Tabasco
1 package (3 ounces) seasoned tomato-salad-gelatin mix	½ cup diced pared cucumber
1 cup tomato juice	½ cup diced green pepper
3 tablespoons red-wine vinegar	¼ cup finely chopped onion
	½ teaspoon snipped fresh chives

1. Pour the boiling water over gelatin in medium-size bowl; stir to dissolve gelatin. Add tomato juice, vinegar, and Tabasco.

2. Set bowl in ice cubes. Let stand, stirring occasionally, until mixture is consistency of unbeaten egg white—about 25 minutes.

3. Stir in cucumber, pepper, onion, and chives. Turn into 4 individual serving dishes.

4. Refrigerate until firm—at least 1 hour.

Makes about 4 cups; 4 servings.

Creamy Lobster Soup

1 can (5 ounces) lobster meat, drained	1 teaspoon prepared mustard
1 small unpared cucumber, diced	1 teaspoon sugar
½ bunch watercress	3 cups buttermilk
	Salt to taste
1 spray fresh dill, cut in pieces	Fresh chives, chopped

1. Place lobster, cucumber, watercress, dill, mustard, sugar, and 2 cups buttermilk in blender container.

2. Blend at high speed, covered, about 10 seconds, or until ingredients are in fine pieces.

3. Add remaining buttermilk and salt; blend 5 seconds.

4. Refrigerate until well chilled. Serve topped with chives.

Makes 4 cups; 4 servings.

Chilled Pea-Potato Soup

1 can (10½ ounces) condensed chicken broth, undiluted	1 can (10¼ ounces) frozen condensed cream of potato soup
2 packages (10-ounce size) frozen green peas	¼ teaspoon salt

1½ cups heavy cream
¼ teaspoon Tabasco

1 tablespoon prepared
   horseradish
8 bacon-flavored crackers

1. In 2-cup measure, combine chicken broth with water to make 2 cups.

2. In medium-size saucepan, combine peas and broth. Bring to boiling; reduce heat; simmer 5 to 7 minutes, or until peas are tender.

3. Meanwhile, place unopened can of cream of potato soup in hot water, to start thawing.

4. Remove pea mixture from heat. Add cream of potato soup and salt; stir until blended.

5. Place half of mixture at a time in electric-blender container; cover; blend, at high speed, 1 to 2 minutes, or until smooth. Pour into large bowl. (Or place in a large mixing bowl, and beat with electric mixer, at low speed, until smooth.)

6. Stir in 1 cup cream and the Tabasco. Refrigerate until thoroughly chilled—at least 3 hours.

7. Just before serving, whip remaining cream; fold in horseradish. Spoon onto crackers.

8. Ladle soup into bouillon cups. Float a cracker on each.

Makes about 2 quarts; 8 servings.

Chilled Salmon Bisque

1 can (1 pound) red salmon
1 small onion, chopped
½ cup chopped green pepper
½ clove garlic, crushed
1 tablespoon butter or
   margarine
2 cups light cream
¼ cup snipped fresh dill

¼ teaspoon Worcestershire
   sauce
¼ teaspoon salt
⅛ teaspoon pepper
2 tablespoons dry sherry
1 tablespoon lemon juice

Lemon wedges

1. Drain salmon; remove and discard skin and large bones.

2. In medium-size skillet, sauté onion, green pepper, and garlic in hot butter until golden—about 5 minutes.

3. Combine salmon, vegetable mixture, cream, dill, Worcestershire, salt, and pepper in electric-blender container; cover; blend, at high speed, 1 minute, or until smooth. Turn into medium-size bowl.

4. Refrigerate, covered, until very well chilled—4 or 5 hours.

5. When ready to serve, stir in sherry and lemon juice. Serve in bouillon cups, with a wedge of lemon.

Makes 8 cups; 8 servings.

Senegalese Soup

1 medium-size onion, chopped	2 cans (10½-ounce size) condensed chicken broth, undiluted
1 medium-size carrot, pared and diced	1 tablespoon almond paste
1 stalk celery, sliced	1 tablespoon red-currant jelly
3 tablespoons butter or margarine	10 whole cloves
2 tablespoons curry powder	1 cinnamon stick
1½ tablespoons flour	1½ cups heavy cream
1 tablespoon tomato paste	2 tablespoons shredded coconut

1. In large saucepan, sauté onion, carrot, and celery in hot butter until golden—about 5 minutes. Remove from heat.

2. Stir in curry powder and flour until well blended. Add tomato paste; cook, stirring, 1 minute.

3. Gradually stir in chicken broth and 2 cups water; bring to boiling, stirring constantly. Stir in almond paste and jelly; add cloves and cinnamon stick; simmer, uncovered and stirring occasionally, ½ hour.

4. Strain; cool. Then refrigerate until very well chilled—several hours or overnight.

5. When ready to serve, skim off any fat from surface. Blend in cream. Serve in bouillon cups. Top each serving with coconut.

Makes about 2 quarts; 8 to 10 servings.

Cold Fresh-Tomato Cream Soup

1 pound tomatoes	1 cup heavy cream
1 can (10½ ounces) condensed onion soup, undiluted	Thin midget-dill-pickle slices

1. Pour boiling water over tomatoes; let stand 1 minute; drain. Cover with cold water; drain. Carefully peel skin; cut out stems.

2. Blend tomatoes, covered, in blender, to make a puree. Measure 2 cups. Discard the rest.

3. Return 2 cups puree to blender. Add onion soup; at low speed, blend, covered, until well combined.

4. Add cream; blend again to combine. Refrigerate until very well chilled—about 2 hours.

5. To serve: Turn soup into chilled mugs. Top each serving with a few pickle slices.

Makes about 1½ quarts; 4 to 6 servings.

III

Salads as a Main Course

❀ ❀ ❀

Do you have a secret conviction you could be a great artist, given the opportunity? Is your favorite daydream one in which you modestly watch them take down the *Mona Lisa* and replace it with the oil portrait you did of your enigmatic Aunt Mildred? The truth is you don't need paints, a canvas, or an atelier in Paris to demonstrate your flair for composition and color. Just put together a salad.

Salads can be artistic triumphs. Colorwise, they can rival any palette—consider the pale pink of a salmon mousse rimmed with lime green cucumber dressing or the rainbow impact of a fruit salad bursting with crimson strawberries, golden peaches, pineapple, and blueberries.

Salads acknowledge textures, too. In a mixed-greens bowl you might contrast the curly leaves of escarole with the stiff, ribbed leaves of romaine and the soft, smooth ones of Bibb.

Finally, salads offer no curbs to creativity. If you choose to combine slivers of chicken with cubes of ham and cheese and toss them with lettuce and black olives, you may do so. Just as salads know no season, neither do they know any limitations.

72

Well, almost no limitations. There are certain things you wouldn't want to do with a salad. Such as serve one of those lunch-counter arrangements we all know so well—that slice or two of tasteless tomato on wilted lettuce, topped with gummy, orange-colored dressing. And we hope you wouldn't want to serve any of those coy combinations designed to look like something they're not—a banana "candle," for example, with a maraschino-cherry flame and a pineapple-cream cheese "candle holder."

While we're discussing salad don'ts, let's include one more: *never* drown a salad with dressing. Salad dressing should be added at the last moment and with a light hand. Just enough to coat each lettuce leaf and ingredient lightly. You can always add more if it's needed, but there's no way to rescue a salad lost in a sea of oil and vinegar or mayonnaise.

When planning a main-course salad, you'll discover you have a wide choice. There are innumerable combinations of greens. There are tempting combinations of fruit. There are seafood salads, meat salads, chicken salads, vegetable salads, and potato and pasta salads. And the selection doesn't stop there—there are molded, refrigerated, and frozen variations.

Let's talk first about green salads, since they rank high in popularity, and when served with rolls, a beverage, and dessert, they make an ideal main dish. They can easily be extended by adding slices of salami or bologna and hard-cooked eggs cut in quarters. Incidentally, when serving a main-course salad, plan on approximately one and one-half servings per person and remember to allow for second servings.

It is important to know the different kinds of salad greens so that you can use them in combinations. Iceberg lettuce, with its large head and crisp, brittle leaves, and Boston, with its greener, smoother leaves and loosely-formed head, are durable. Bibb lettuce has soft-textured, cup-shaped green leaves. Leaf lettuce never forms into heads but has the same sweet, delicate flavor Bibb possesses. Sharp-flavored romaine comes in elongated heads with stiff, thick-ribbed leaves. Curly endive or chicory is a narrow-leaf lettuce with feathery curls on heavy ribs. The exterior is dark green, the heart pale yellow and slightly bitter in flavor. Escarole, also with a pungent flavor, has broad, twisted wavy leaves, dark green with white midribs. That sophisticated import French or Belgian endive has creamy cylindrical leaves tapering to a point. Young spinach leaves, dark green in color, add a tangy quality to salad. And watercress, a long-stemmed plant with small, dark-green leaflets and a peppery flavor, is especially useful for garnishing.

Salad greens should be in perfect condition. Discard soiled, rusty, and wilted leaves. Rinse under cold water. You can freshen up "tired" heads by cutting off the roots and plunging the cut ends into ice-cold water for a half hour. Gently pat leaves dry between paper towels (if left wet, they'll dilute the salad dressing) and store them in a plastic bag in the refrigerator. Always tear, never cut lettuce leaves—tearing allows for better absorption of the dressing. The exception is endive, which may be cut into bite-size pieces or stripped off into separate leaves.

A tossed salad cannot be made in advance of a dinner party, but you can save time by preparing the ingredients, then storing them separately from each other between layers of waxed paper in one big bowl. When you finally do combine them for serving, add the tomato wedges, if any, at the last moment so they won't dilute the salad dressing.

Your choice of salad bowl will contribute to the eye appeal and the tastiness of your salad. It should be large enough to allow for a vigorous tossing. Wooden bowls are a classic choice but they require special care. If uncoated, wipe dry with damp paper toweling. If coated, you may rinse out the bowl, but don't soak it with the dishes; detergents will eat through the coating. Don't nest wooden bowls that are still damp. And never put them in direct sunlight or heat to dry; you'll wind up with a bowl full of splits and cracks.

One last warning: a salad may look beautifully fresh and crisp, but without the proper dressing it can be a failure. Tart or tangy, spicy or sweet, rich or creamy—the dressing makes the salad.

French dressings, both clear and creamy, are a mixture of oil, vinegar or lemon juice, and seasonings. The clear dressings separate and must be shaken at each use; creamy dressings do not separate because they are homogenized.

Mayonnaise is a creamy dressing made by beating oil slowly into egg yolk (or whole egg) with vinegar or lemon juice and seasonings.

Salad dressing is similar to mayonnaise but with oil and egg in smaller proportions. Its flavor is usually tangier than that of mayonnaise.

Cooked or boiled dressing is high in egg and low in fat; it is made by cooking a white sauce-egg base to which vinegar, butter or margarine, and seasonings are added.

In general, French dressings are best with green, vegetable, and fruit salads. Mayonnaise and salad dressings heighten the flavor of meat, seafood, egg, and molded salads. Cooked dressings mate well with potato and pasta salads and, if sweetened, are excellent as fruit toppings.

A hot summer day—or any day for a dieter—is the right time for a main-dish fruit salad. With or without cream cheese or cottage cheese, fruit salads can satisfy the hungry diner—particularly if several kinds of fruit are used and a basket of breadsticks and rolls is at hand. (In an emergency, combine canned and fresh fruits, but only in an emergency if you want to keep your merit badge.) Use fairly uniform pieces of fruit and make certain the fruit flavors blend together pleasantly. To keep fresh fruit from darkening, slice at the last moment and sprinkle the sections with lemon juice. As a variation from lettuce, try scooped-out pineapple shells or melon halves piled high with fruit.

All salads have charm but it is the molded salad that is the special delight of the hostess. That's because she can make it a day ahead and have plenty of time left to attend to her other chores. This type of salad is also an admirable way of utilizing leftover vegetables, fruit, meat, or chicken. And it can be made in one large mold, in individual small molds, or cut in squares from a pan.

These shimmering, appetizing charmers are easy to make: just be certain to follow the package directions for dissolving the gelatin that is their base. Flavored and unflavored gelatins are dissolved by different methods.

When you have made the gelatin, allow it to thicken to an egg white consistency before adding fruits, vegetables, meat, or seafood. You can speed up the thickening process by putting the gelatin mixture in a bowl of ice and water or in your freezer compartment for a short time. For layering, allow each layer of gelatin to set before you add the next one.

Some faint-hearted cooks hesitate to serve molded salads because they fear they won't be able to unmold them easily. The trick is to dip the mold in warm, not hot water to the depth of the contents, then to loosen the edge of the salad all around with the tip of a paring knife. Put a plate on top of the mold, hold tightly, and invert both plate and mold. Shake the mold slightly and *voilà!* One molded salad is free.

Garnishing a salad can be as much fun as picking out a new shade of lipstick or a pair of earrings. There are countless possibilities; all you need is imagination. Consider onion rings, crumbled blue cheese, watercress, bits of bacon, nuts, sliced eggs or crumbled egg yolks, carrot curls, parsley, radish "roses," or pickles; and for fruit salads, chopped nuts, raisins, chopped maraschino cherries, fresh mint leaves, shredded coconut.

Croutons for green salads, like those for soup, are easy to make: without removing crusts, cut white, wheat, or rye bread into cubes, and toast them on a baking sheet in a slow, 300° F. oven, turning occasionally, until lightly browned. Melt butter and a garlic clove in a skillet, removing the garlic when it is brown. Add the bread cubes, toss until coated. Keep in a covered jar in the refrigerator, heating just before use.

A neighbor of ours who serves salads as a main course at least once a week tells us she has a favorite trick. She serves two small salads on the dinner plate, one a fruit, the other a meat, fish, or chicken salad. That way, everybody's happy. She's also the cook who tosses a green salad in the kitchen and transfers it to an oversized brandy snifter for serving at the table. It never fails to impress her family and friends.

Roast-Beef-and-Mushroom Salad

2 tablespoons butter or margarine
½ teaspoon seasoned salt

¼ teaspoon onion powder
1 cup bite-size shredded-corn biscuits

Dressing

½ cup bottled clear Russian dressing
1 tablespoon prepared mustard
½ teaspoon Worcestershire sauce

½ package (10-ounce size) frozen asparagus spears

1 quart bite-size pieces escarole
2 cups bite-size pieces Boston lettuce
½ pound cooked roast beef, cut into thin strips
1 pimiento, cut into thin strips
½ cup washed, thinly sliced raw mushrooms

1. Melt butter in small skillet. Stir in seasoned salt and onion powder. Add corn cereal; sauté 5 minutes, stirring constantly; set aside. Do not refrigerate.

2. Make Dressing: In jar with tight-fitting lid, combine Russian dressing, mustard, and Worcestershire sauce; shake vigorously, to mix well.

3. Cook asparagus as package label directs; drain. Cut spears in half crosswise. Add just enough dressing to coat asparagus pieces well.

4. Refrigerate asparagus, rest of dressing, and remaining salad ingredients until well chilled—about 2 hours.

5. Just before serving, toss escarole with Boston lettuce in salad bowl. Arrange asparagus, beef, pimiento, and mushrooms attractively over greens.

6. Arrange corn cereal around top of salad.

7. Add dressing; toss to combine well.

Makes 6 servings.

Frankfurter Salad Bowl

1 package (9 ounces) frozen French-style green beans
1 pound frankfurters
3 tablespoons olive or salad oil
1 cup sliced onion
1 cup thinly sliced celery
½ cup green-pepper strips

1 clove garlic, crushed
1½ teaspoons salt
¼ teaspoon pepper
½ teaspoon dried oregano leaves
⅓ cup tarragon vinegar
½ cup packaged croutons

1. Cook beans as package label directs; drain.

2. Cut frankfurters into 1-inch pieces. In hot oil in medium-size skillet, sauté frankfurters until golden—about 5 minutes.

3. Combine beans and frankfurters with onion, celery, green pepper, garlic, salt, pepper, oregano, and vinegar; toss to combine.

4. Refrigerate until well chilled—about 2 hours. Just before serving, toss salad with croutons.

Makes 4 to 6 servings.

Wilted-Lettuce Salad with Franks

4 cups iceberg lettuce in bite-size pieces
2 cups Bibb lettuce in bite-size pieces

1 tablespoon chopped chives
4 slices bacon
4 frankfurters, cut into ¼-inch-thick slices

¼ cup vinegar	¼ teaspoon salt
½ clove garlic, crushed	¼ teaspoon pepper
1½ teaspoons sugar	¼ teaspoon dry mustard

1. In salad bowl, combine lettuce and chives. Refrigerate, covered, until ready to use.

2. In skillet, sauté bacon until crisp; remove. Add frankfurters; sauté until browned on all sides. Remove from heat.

3. Remove frankfurters with slotted utensil. Crumble bacon, and coarsely chop half of frankfurters. Add bacon and all frankfurters to greens in salad bowl.

4. Measure drippings; return 3 to 4 tablespoons to skillet. Add vinegar, garlic, sugar, salt, pepper, and mustard; bring to boiling, stirring.

5. Pour over salad. Toss until all greens are coated with dressing.

6. Serve at once.

Makes 6 servings.

Ham Salad with Dill Dressing

Dressing

| ¾ cup dairy sour cream | 1 tablespoon snipped fresh dill |
| ¼ cup bottled clear French dressing | |

Salad

1 package (9 ounces) frozen artichoke hearts	1 can (1 pound) fully cooked ham
1 can (1 pound) peeled, whole white potatoes	¼ cup sliced sweet gherkins
	Salad greens

1. Make Dressing: In medium-size bowl, combine all dressing ingredients, mixing well. Refrigerate, covered, at least 1 hour.

2. Meanwhile, make Salad: Cook artichoke hearts as package label directs. Drain well, and halve lengthwise. Refrigerate, covered, along with potatoes until they are well chilled—about 1 hour.

3. Just before serving, remove and discard gelatin and excess fat from ham. Then cut ham into ½-inch cubes.

4. Drain potatoes; cut each potato into 4 slices.

5. In large bowl, toss artichoke hearts with ham cubes, potato slices, and gherkins. Add dressing; toss lightly to mix well.

6. To serve: Surround edge of salad bowl with salad greens. Mound salad high in center.

Makes 6 to 8 servings.

Ham-and-Swiss Salad Bowl

½ package (9-ounce size) frozen French-style green beans

Dressing
½ cup salad oil
¼ cup cider vinegar
1 tablespoon drained prepared horseradish
1 teaspoon dry mustard
½ teaspoon salt
Few drops Tabasco

3 cups bite-size pieces Boston lettuce
2 tablespoons snipped chives
¼ pound cooked ham, cut into thin strips
¼ pound natural Swiss cheese, cut into thin strips
3 hard-cooked eggs, quartered

3 cups bite-size pieces romaine

1. Cook beans as package label directs; drain. Turn into shallow dish.

2. Make Dressing: Combine salad oil, vinegar, horseradish, mustard, salt, and Tabasco in jar with tight-fitting lid. Shake vigorously, to mix well.

3. Pour just enough dressing over beans to coat well. Refrigerate beans, rest of dressing, and remainder of ingredients, covered, until well chilled—about 2 hours.

4. Just before serving, toss romaine, Boston lettuce, and chives together in large salad bowl.

5. Arrange beans, ham, cheese, and eggs over greens. Shake dressing; pour over salad. Toss to combine.

Makes 6 servings.

Chef's Salad de Luxe

Cheese Dressing
½ cup salad oil
¼ cup mayonnaise or cooked salad dressing
1 jar (5 ounces) sharp cheese spread
3 tablespoons white vinegar
1 teaspoon Worcestershire sauce
½ teaspoon paprika
¼ teaspoon salt

3 bacon slices, halved
4 frankfurters
1 medium-size head iceberg lettuce, torn into bite-size pieces
½ small green pepper, cut into thin strips
1 tomato, cut into wedges
½ medium-size red onion, sliced into thin rings

1. Make Cheese Dressing: In small bowl, combine oil, mayonnaise, cheese spread, vinegar, Worcestershire, paprika, and salt. Beat, with rotary beater, until well blended. Refrigerate, covered, until well chilled—about 2 hours.

2. Meanwhile, in medium-size skillet, sauté bacon until crisp. Drain bacon well on paper towels, reserving 1 tablespoon drippings.

3. Halve frankfurters lengthwise; cut each half into quarters.

4. In reserved bacon drippings, sauté frankfurters 5 minutes, stirring occasionally; drain.

5. Refrigerate bacon, frankfurters, and remaining salad ingredients until well chilled.

6. Just before serving, turn lettuce into a large salad bowl; arrange bacon, frankfurters, green pepper, tomato, and onion attractively over lettuce.

7. Toss salad to mix well. Serve with Cheese Dressing.
Makes 6 servings.

California Chef's Salad

Dressing
½ cup salad oil
⅓ cup lemon juice
1 teaspoon grated onion
1 teaspoon sugar

½ teaspoon salt
½ teaspoon dried oregano leaves
¼ teaspoon dried thyme leaves

1 large navel orange
4 cups bite-size pieces Chinese
cabbage
2 cups bite-size pieces spinach

1 cup cooked chicken, cut into
thin strips
¼ pound natural Muenster
cheese, cut into thin strips
6 pitted ripe olives, halved

1. Make Dressing: Combine all dressing ingredients in jar with tight-fitting lid; shake vigorously, to combine. Refrigerate until well chilled—about 2 hours.

2. Peel orange, removing all white membrane. Cut crosswise into thick slices; cut each slice in half.

3. Refrigerate orange slices, along with rest of ingredients, until well chilled.

4. Just before serving, toss cabbage with spinach in a large salad bowl.

5. Arrange orange slices, chicken, cheese, and olives over greens.

6. Shake dressing; pour over salad. Toss gently to combine.

Makes 6 servings.

Ripe-Olive Salad Bowl

Dressing

⅔ cup olive oil
⅓ cup lemon juice
¼ cup chopped fresh mint
1 clove garlic, crushed
1¼ teaspoons salt
¼ teaspoon pepper

1 head iceberg lettuce, washed
and chilled
¼ head chicory, washed and
chilled
½ head romaine, washed and
chilled

1 Belgian endive, washed and
chilled
1 medium-size cucumber, pared
and sliced
½ medium-size green pepper,
cut into thin strips
1 bunch scallions, cut into
½-inch pieces
¼ cup chopped parsley
1 cup pitted ripe olives
1½ cups crumbled feta cheese
1 can (2 ounces) anchovy
fillets, drained

1. Make Dressing: In jar with tight-fitting lid, combine olive oil, lemon juice, mint, garlic, salt, and pepper; shake vigorously. Refrigerate until ready to use.

2. Tear lettuce, chicory, romaine, and endive into bite-size pieces into large salad bowl. (This may be done several hours before serving. Store the torn greens, covered, in the refrigerator.)

3. Add cucumber, green pepper, scallions, parsley, olives, cheese, and anchovies.

4. Shake dressing. Pour about ½ cup over salad; toss lightly. Pass remaining dressing.

Makes 8 servings.

Salamagundi Salad Bowl

French Dressing

¾ cup salad or olive oil
¼ cup red-wine vinegar
2 tablespoons catsup
1½ tablespoons sugar
1½ teaspoons salt
⅛ teaspoon paprika

Dash pepper
½ teaspoon lemon juice
¼ teaspoon prepared mustard
¼ teaspoon prepared horseradish
Dash Tabasco

Garlic Croutons

¼ cup salad oil
½ clove garlic, crushed
1½ cups fresh bread cubes

4 cups bite-size pieces crisp spinach
4 cups bite-size pieces crisp Boston lettuce

¾ pound natural Swiss cheese
½ pound sliced salami
1 can (7 ounces) water chestnuts

3 hard-cooked eggs, sliced

1. Make French Dressing: In jar with tight-fitting lid, combine all dressing ingredients; shake vigorously to combine. Refrigerate until ready to use.

2. Make Garlic Croutons: In skillet, combine salad oil and garlic; heat slowly. Add bread cubes, and sauté until golden brown on all sides. Drain on paper towels, and set aside.

3. Just before serving, cut Swiss cheese into ½-inch cubes. Cut each salami slice into 6 wedges. Drain water chestnuts, and slice.

4. Place spinach and lettuce in salad bowl; toss lightly. Add cheese, salami, water chestnuts, and croutons.

5. Shake dressing well; pour over salad. Toss until well coated. Garnish with egg slices.

Makes 6 to 8 servings.

Caesar Salad

1 clove garlic, crushed	12 anchovy fillets, drained and
¾ cup salad oil	chopped
¼ cup olive oil	½ clove garlic
2 cups French-bread cubes	1 medium-size head romaine,
(½-inch)	washed and chilled
1½ teaspoons salt	1 medium-size head iceberg
½ teaspoon dry mustard	lettuce, washed and chilled
½ teaspoon freshly ground	½ cup grated Parmesan cheese
black pepper	¼ cup crumbled blue cheese
1 tablespoon Worcestershire	2 raw eggs*
sauce	¼ cup lemon juice

1. In jar with tight-fitting lid, combine crushed clove garlic with salad oil and olive oil. Refrigerate 1 hour.

2. In ¼ cup garlic-oil mixture in medium-size skillet, sauté bread cubes until brown on all sides. Set aside.

3. To remaining garlic-oil mixture in jar, add salt, mustard, pepper, Worcestershire, and anchovies. Shake dressing vigorously. Refrigerate until needed.

4. Just before serving, rub inside of large wooden salad bowl with cut side of ½ clove garlic; discard garlic.

5. Tear greens in bite-size pieces into salad bowl. (Greens should measure about 4 quarts.)

6. Shake dressing. Pour over greens. Sprinkle with Parmesan and blue cheese. Toss to coat evenly.

7. Break eggs over middle of salad. Pour lemon juice directly over eggs; toss well.

8. Add bread cubes; toss again. Serve at once.

Makes 8 to 10 servings.

---

*If desired, cook eggs 1 minute in boiling water.

Chicken Salad

1 (5- to 5½-pound size) ready-to-cook roasting chicken
2 large carrots, pared and cut into 1-inch pieces
2 stalks celery, cut into 1-inch pieces
1 large onion, sliced
6 whole black peppercorns
2 teaspoons salt
1 bay leaf

1 cup mayonnaise or cooked salad dressing
2 tablespoons lemon juice
2 tablespoons milk or light cream
1½ teaspoons salt
Dash pepper
3 or 4 crisp large celery stalks

Crisp lettuce
Watercress
Tomato wedges

1. Remove giblets and neck from chicken. Then rinse chicken well under cold water. Place, breast side down, in an 8-quart kettle.

2. Add carrot, cut-up celery, onion, whole peppercorns, 2 teaspoons salt, the bay leaf, and 1 quart water.

3. Bring to boiling over high heat. Reduce heat, and simmer, covered, about 2 hours, or until chicken is tender. (After 1 hour, carefully turn chicken with wooden spoons.) Remove kettle from heat.

4. Let stand, uncovered and frequently spooning broth in kettle over chicken, 1 hour, or until cool enough to handle. Lift out chicken. Strain broth, and refrigerate, covered, to use as desired.

5. Cut legs, thighs, and wings from chicken. Remove skin. Then remove meat from bones in as large pieces as possible. Set aside.

6. Pull skin from remaining chicken. With sharp knife, cut between the breastbone and meat, removing breast meat in large piece. Then check carefully, and remove any additional meat. Refrigerate, covered, to chill—about 1½ hours.

7. Make Salad: In large bowl, combine mayonnaise, lemon juice, milk, salt, and pepper; stir until blended.

8. Cut celery, on the diagonal, into thin slices, to measure 2 cups. Add to dressing in bowl.

9. Cut large pieces of chicken meat into 1-inch pieces; there should be almost 5 cups. Add all meat to dressing. Toss lightly, to coat well.

10. Refrigerate, covered, until serving time—at least 1 hour.

11. To serve: Spoon salad into attractive bowl; garnish with lettuce, watercress, and tomato wedges.

Makes 6 to 8 servings.

Chicken Waldorf Salad

Chicken Salad (see p. 84)
2 cups coarsely diced red apple

¾ cup broken walnuts

1. Prepare Chicken Salad, reducing sliced celery to 1 cup.
2. Add apple to dressing as soon as apple is cut, to prevent darkening.
3. Add walnuts and celery; toss lightly.
4. Garnish with lettuce leaves and watercress.
Makes 8 servings.

Chicken Fruit Salad

Chicken Salad (see p. 84)
1 cup coarsely diced pared
   cucumber
1 can (13¼ ounces) frozen
   pineapple chunks, thawed
   and drained

¼ cup toasted slivered almonds
   (optional)

1. Prepare Chicken Salad, reducing sliced celery to 1 cup.
2. Add diced cucumber with celery.
3. Just before serving, add pineapple chunks.
4. Garnish bowl with lettuce and watercress. Sprinkle with almonds,
if desired.
Makes 8 servings.

Chicken-and-Ham Salad Véronique

Chicken

4 (12-ounce size) broiler-fryer
   breasts
2 stalks celery, with leaves
1 medium-size onion, peeled
   and sliced
1 tablespoon salt
½ teaspoon poultry seasoning

½ teaspoon curry powder
6 whole black peppercorns

1 medium-size head iceberg
   lettuce, washed and chilled
1 head (½ pound) chicory,
   washed and chilled

Sour-Cream Dressing

1 cup mayonnaise or cooked salad dressing	½ teaspoon salt
½ cup dairy sour cream	3 cups diced cooked ham (¾ pound)
½ cup prepared chutney, finely chopped	1 pound seedless green grapes (2½ to 3 cups)
1 tablespoon lemon juice	

1. Prepare Chicken: Wash chicken; place in large kettle. Add 1 quart water, the celery, onion, salt, poultry seasoning, curry powder, and black peppercorns; bring to boiling. Reduce heat, and simmer, covered, 35 minutes, or until tender.

2. Remove chicken from broth; remove skin and bones. Refrigerate, covered, until well chilled—at least 3 hours, or overnight. (Refrigerate broth; use as desired.)

3. Just before serving, cut chicken in bite-size pieces—you should have about 4 cups.

4. Tear lettuce and chicory into bite-size pieces in salad bowl.

5. Make Sour-Cream Dressing: In large bowl, combine all dressing ingredients. Add chicken, ham, and grapes; mix well. Spoon over greens.

Makes 8 servings.

Turkey-and-Avocado Salad Bowl

Dressing

⅔ cup bottled Italian-style dressing	3 tablespoons sliced scallions
1 wedge (2 ounces) blue cheese, crumbled	¼ pound cooked turkey, cut into thin strips
1 tablespoon drained bottled capers	¼ pound spiced ham, cut into thin strips
1 medium-size head escarole, torn into bite-size pieces	1 medium-size carrot, pared and cut into thin strips
	1 small green- or black-skinned avocado, peeled and cubed

1. Make Dressing: Combine all dressing ingredients in jar with tight-fitting lid; shake vigorously, to mix well.

2. Refrigerate, along with rest of salad ingredients, until well chilled—about 2 hours.

3. Just before serving, toss escarole and scallions in salad bowl. Arrange turkey, ham, carrot, and avocado attractively over greens.

4. Add dressing; toss to combine well.

Makes 6 servings.

French Potato Salad

3 pounds waxy or new potatoes	1 tablespoon chopped fresh
¼ cup wine vinegar	tarragon or 1 teaspoon dried
1½ teaspoons salt	tarragon leaves
1 teaspoon freshly ground	2 teaspoons chopped fresh
pepper	chervil or ½ teaspoon dried
3 tablespoons canned	chervil leaves
condensed beef consommé,	1½ tablespoons chopped parsley
undiluted	1 tablespoon chopped chives
⅓ cup dry white wine	¾ cup salad or olive oil

1. Cook potatoes, covered, in enough boiling, salted water to cover, 30 minutes, or just until fork-tender.

2. Drain; peel; slice while still warm into ¼-inch-thick slices into salad bowl.

3. In bowl or jar with tight-fitting lid, combine vinegar and rest of ingredients; mix very well.

4. Pour over warm potatoes; toss gently to coat with liquid. Serve warm, or let cool and refrigerate. Before serving, toss gently again.

Makes 8 servings.

German Potato Salad

3½ pounds medium-size potatoes (about 10)	2 tablespoons butter or margarine
1 cup chopped onion	1½ teaspoons salt
½ pound bacon, diced	¼ teaspoon pepper
2 tablespoons flour	½ cup cider vinegar
¼ cup sugar	1 cup dairy sour cream
	Chopped parsley

1. Cook potatoes, covered, in salted boiling water to cover, 35 to 40 minutes, or until fork-tender. Peel warm potatoes; slice; add onion.

2. In large skillet, cook bacon; remove from heat. Lift out with slotted spoon, and set aside. Pour off fat; return ¼ cup to skillet.

3. Stir flour into fat in skillet. Add sugar, butter, salt, pepper, vinegar, and 1 cup water. Bring to boil, stirring. Remove from heat; add sour cream.

4. Add potatoes, onion, half of bacon; toss gently. Sprinkle with rest of bacon and the parsley. Serve warm or cold.

Makes 10 servings.

Mashed-Potato Salad

4 pounds pared medium-size potatoes (about 8 to 10)	3 medium-size tomatoes, coarsely chopped
1½ teaspoons salt	½ cup chopped green-onion tops
¼ teaspoon pepper	
¼ cup cider vinegar	¾ cup chopped green pepper
1 to 1½ cups mayonnaise	1 cup chopped celery
6 hard-cooked eggs, coarsely chopped	

1. In large kettle, cook potatoes in 1 inch boiling salted water, covered, until tender—about 30 minutes; drain well. With potato masher, mash right in pan until light and smooth.

2. Add salt, pepper, vinegar, and mayonnaise; mix well.

3. Add eggs and rest of ingredients; toss gently to combine. Mound in salad bowl. Serve warm or cold.

Makes 10 servings.

Avocado-Walnut Salad

Dressing

¾ cup salad oil	¼ teaspoon pepper
¼ cup lemon juice	1 tablespoon grated onion
1½ teaspoons salt	

3½ quarts bite-size pieces mixed greens (iceberg or Boston lettuce, romaine, and chicory)

1 Belgian endive, cut into 1-inch-thick slices
2 large avocados
¼ cup coarsely chopped walnuts

1. Make Dressing: In a jar with a tight-fitting lid, combine oil, lemon juice, salt, pepper, and onion. Cover, and shake vigorously a few minutes. Refrigerate until chilled—at least 2 hours.

2. Meanwhile, combine mixed greens and endive in a salad bowl. Refrigerate, covered, until chilled—about 1 hour.

3. Just before serving, cut avocados in half lengthwise; remove pits; peel, and slice. Add to greens.

4. Add walnuts to dressing; shake vigorously, and pour over greens. Toss until greens are well coated with dressing.

Makes 12 servings.

Fiesta Salad Platter

Green Mayonnaise

1 cup mayonnaise or cooked salad dressing
2 tablespoons lemon juice
2 tablespoons chopped parsley
1 tablespoon chopped chives
1 tablespoon chopped watercress

1 large head cauliflower (2½ pounds)
Boiling water
1 cup milk
1 teaspoon salt
1 bottle (8 ounces) herb-flavored oil-and-vinegar dressing

2 packages (9-ounce size) frozen whole green beans, or 2 cans (15½-ounce size) whole green beans
1 tablespoon butter or margarine
½ cup day-old bread cubes
Boston lettuce
2 large tomatoes, sliced (1 pound)

Pimiento
Dill sprigs

1. Make Green Mayonnaise: In small bowl, combine mayonnaise, lemon juice, parsley, chives, and watercress; mix well. Refrigerate, covered, overnight.

2. Wash cauliflower, and leave whole. Place in large kettle; cover with boiling water. Add milk and salt; boil gently, uncovered, 30 minutes, or just until stem of cauliflower is tender. Drain; then let cool 10 minutes. Place, stem end up, in bowl; pour herb dressing over cauliflower. Refrigerate, covered, overnight.

3. Several hours before serving, cook frozen green beans as package label directs. Drain. (If using canned beans, drain well.) Drain cauliflower, reserving dressing. Place beans in shallow dish with reserved dressing. Refrigerate, covered, along with cauliflower, until needed.

4. In hot butter in small skillet, sauté bread cubes until golden brown. Set aside.

5. To serve: Drain beans. Place cauliflower, stem end down, in center of large platter; place lettuce leaves around edge. Alternate green beans and tomato slices on lettuce leaves. Garnish the beans with bread cubes and the cauliflower with bits of pimiento and dill sprigs. Pass green mayonnaise.

Makes 8 to 10 servings.

Bouillabaisse Salad

Seafood

1 (1-pound size) halibut steak
1 teaspoon salt
½ pound bay scallops
2 (8-ounce size) frozen rock-lobster tails
½ pound shrimp, shelled and deveined

1 package (6½ ounces) frozen king-crab meat, thawed and drained
⅓ cup bottled herb or oil-and-vinegar salad dressing

Pink Mayonnaise

1¼ cups mayonnaise or cooked salad dressing
⅓ cup chili sauce
2 tablespoons vinegar
1 tablespoon chopped parsley
1 teaspoon grated onion

1 teaspoon Worcestershire sauce
1 teaspoon prepared horseradish
Dash cayenne pepper

| 5 cups bite-size pieces crisp romaine | Watercress sprigs |
| 3 cups bite-size pieces crisp chicory | Lemon wedges |

1. Prepare Seafood: Place halibut in large skillet; cover with cold water; add ½ teaspoon salt. Bring to boiling; reduce heat, and simmer, covered, 10 minutes, or until fish flakes easily with fork. Remove, and drain.

2. Add scallops to same water; bring just to boiling; simmer, covered, 2 minutes. Remove, and drain.

3. Meanwhile, in medium-size saucepan, bring 5 cups water to boiling with ½ teaspoon salt. Add lobster; return to boiling. Reduce heat, and simmer, covered, 12 minutes. Remove, and drain. Add shrimp to same water; simmer 5 minutes. Remove, and drain.

4. Break halibut into large chunks, discarding skin and bones. Remove lobster from shell, and cut into large pieces. Cut crab meat into large pieces, removing membrane.

5. Arrange halibut, scallops, lobster, shrimp, and crab meat in shallow dish. Drizzle with herb salad dressing. Refrigerate, covered, until well chilled—3 to 4 hours.

6. Make Pink Mayonnaise: In medium-size bowl, combine all dressing ingredients; beat well with rotary beater. Refrigerate, covered.

7. To serve: Place romaine and chicory in large, shallow serving dish. Drain seafood, and toss with Pink Mayonnaise. Spoon over greens. Garnish with watercress and lemon wedges.

Makes 8 servings.

Note: If using sea scallops, cut into quarters; cook as above. Cook frozen scallops 1 minute longer.

Salade Niçoise

2 cans (7-ounce size) tuna, drained	1 can (1 pound) whole new potatoes, drained and sliced
2 tablespoons sliced stuffed green olives	1 can (8 ounces) French-style green beans, drained
½ cup bottled herb-and-garlic salad dressing	1 teaspoon instant minced onion

1 can (8¼ ounces) small whole beets	½ cup grated pared carrot
¾ cup thinly sliced cucumber	1 tomato, quartered
⅛ teaspoon salt	1 can (2 ounces) anchovy fillets, drained
⅛ teaspoon sugar	
Crisp lettuce	2 hard-cooked eggs, halved

1. In small bowl, break up tuna with fork; gently toss with olives and 2 tablespoons salad dressing; refrigerate, covered.

2. In bowl, toss sliced potatoes and green beans with ¼ cup dressing and the instant minced onion; refrigerate, covered, until ready for serving.

3. Toss beets with remaining dressing; refrigerate.

4. Sprinkle sliced cucumber with salt and sugar; refrigerate.

5. To serve: Arrange lettuce in large salad bowl. Mound tuna mixture in center. Arrange mounds of potatoes and beans, beets, carrot, and cucumber around tuna. Garnish with tomato, anchovies, and eggs. Bring to table, and toss gently. Pass more dressing, if desired.

Makes 4 to 6 servings.

Codfish Salad

3 packages (1-pound size) salt codfish	1 tablespoon chopped onion
	1 tablespoon chopped shallots
9 small new potatoes, scrubbed and unpared (about 1¼ pounds)	1 garlic clove, finely chopped
	¼ cup chopped parsley

Dressing

¾ cup salad oil	⅛ teaspoon Worcestershire sauce
¼ cup red-wine vinegar	
½ teaspoon pepper	

1. Freshen codfish as package label directs.

2. In 3-quart saucepan, cook potatoes in 1 inch of boiling water, covered, 10 minutes. Remove from heat.

3. Arrange codfish on potatoes. Cook, covered and over medium heat, about 20 minutes, or until potatoes are tender and fish flakes easily with fork.

4. Carefully lift off fish. Drain potatoes. While still hot, pare; cut into small pieces. Separate fish into small pieces.

5. With fork, lightly toss potatoes with fish, onion, shallots, garlic, and parsley until well combined.

6. Make Dressing: In small jar with tight-fitting lid, combine all dressing ingredients; shake vigorously.

7. Pour dressing over salad; mix gently to combine. Serve warm.

Makes 4 to 6 servings.

Curried-Seafood Salad Bowl

1 package (7 ounces) frozen shelled, deveined shrimp	1 can (8¾ ounces) pineapple tidbits

Dressing

¾ cup mayonnaise or cooked salad dressing	5 cups shredded iceberg lettuce
2 tablespoons chopped prepared chutney	½ cup coarsely chopped watercress
1 tablespoon cider vinegar	1 package (6 ounces) frozen king-crab meat, thawed and
½ teaspoon curry powder	drained
	½ cup salted peanuts

1. Cook shrimp as package label directs; drain. Refrigerate until well chilled.

2. Drain pineapple, reserving 2 tablespoons liquid for dressing.

3. Make Dressing: In small bowl, combine the reserved pineapple liquid with remaining dressing ingredients, mixing well.

4. Refrigerate pineapple tidbits, dressing, and rest of ingredients until well chilled—about 2 hours.

5. Just before serving, toss lettuce and watercress together in a large salad bowl. Arrange shrimp, pineapple, and crab meat over greens. Sprinkle peanuts over top.

6. Add dressing; toss gently to combine.

Makes 4 servings.

Dilled Fish Salad

1 tablespoon lemon juice
½ teaspoon salt
⅛ teaspoon cayenne
3 tablespoons olive oil
2 tablespoons finely chopped shallots or scallions
2 tablespoons finely chopped fresh dill
2 cups poached sole, chilled and cut into 1- or 2-inch pieces

1 cup homemade mayonnaise or unsweetened commercial mayonnaise
2 to 3 cups romaine or Boston lettuce, thoroughly dried, shredded, and chilled
4 small tomatoes, peeled and sliced
2 hard-cooked eggs, sliced
2 tablespoons capers, drained, washed, and dried

1. In a small mixing bowl, mix together the lemon juice, salt, cayenne, olive oil, shallots or scallions, and 1 tablespoon of the dill. Pour it over the cold fish, and toss gently. Let the fish marinate in this mixture for about 1 hour, turning the pieces over every now and then.

2. Choose a large glass or crystal bowl in which to construct and serve the salad. Combine the marinated fish with its marinade and ½ cup of the mayonnaise. Arrange this mixture on the shredded greens in the salad bowl.

3. Stir remaining 1 tablespoon of dill into the remaining mayonnaise, and spread the mayonnaise over the fish, masking it completely.

4. Alternately overlap the sliced tomatoes and hard-cooked eggs around the edge of the bowl, and sprinkle the capers over the masked fish. Serve chilled.

Makes 4 servings.

Green-Goddess Salad

Green-Goddess Dressing

6 anchovy fillets, chopped
2 tablespoons finely chopped green onion
2 tablespoons snipped chives
¼ cup finely chopped parsley
¼ teaspoon salt

½ teaspoon dry mustard
⅛ teaspoon pepper
¼ cup tarragon vinegar
1 cup mayonnaise or cooked salad dressing

Salad

1 medium-size head Boston lettuce, cored, washed, and chilled	3 cups cubed cooked lobster, crab meat, or chicken, chilled
1 head romaine, washed and chilled	2 medium-size tomatoes, sliced

1. Make Green-Goddess Dressing: In small bowl, combine all dressing ingredients; mix well. Refrigerate, covered, several hours or overnight, to let flavors blend.

2. Just before serving, make Salad: Tear enough greens into bite-size pieces to measure 2 quarts. Turn into salad bowl.

3. Arrange lobster in center of greens. Add dressing; toss to coat lobster and greens well.

4. Garnish with tomato slices.

Makes 8 servings.

Lobster Chef's Salad

2 packages (8-ounce size) frozen rock-lobster tails	½ package (9-ounce size) frozen artichoke hearts

Dressing

½ cup mayonnaise or cooked salad dressing	1 quart bite-size pieces Boston lettuce
¼ cup dairy sour cream	1 tablespoon snipped fresh dill
2 tablespoons tarragon vinegar	¾ cup pared, cubed cucumber
1 teaspoon sugar	
½ teaspoon seasoned salt	½ cup crushed potato chips (optional)

1. Cook lobster tails and artichoke hearts as package labels direct; drain.

2. Remove lobster meat from shells in one piece; cut into cubes. Cut artichoke hearts in halves lengthwise.

3. Refrigerate lobster and artichoke hearts, covered, until well chilled.

4. Meanwhile, make Dressing: Combine all dressing ingredients in small bowl, mixing well. Refrigerate, along with remaining salad ingredients, until well chilled—about 2 hours.

5. Just before serving, toss lettuce with dill in large salad bowl. Arrange the lobster, cucumber, and artichoke hearts attractively over greens.

6. Add dressing; toss to combine well. Serve with crushed potato chips sprinkled over top of salad, if desired.

Makes 6 servings.

Pacific Coast Salad

7 medium-size potatoes (about 2¼ pounds)
1 medium-size onion
1 bottle (8 ounces) Italian-style salad dressing
1 can (7 ounces) solid-pack tuna

1 can (7½ ounces) salmon
1 tablespoon chopped fresh dill

Boston lettuce, washed and chilled

1. Scrub potatoes. Cook in boiling, salted water, covered, just until tender—about 30 minutes. Drain, and let cool slightly.

2. Peel potatoes; then cut into slices ¼ inch thick. Peel onion; slice, and separate into rings.

3. In shallow baking dish, arrange potato slices and onion rings in alternate layers. Pour ¾ cup salad dressing over all. Refrigerate, covered, 3 hours.

4. Meanwhile, drain tuna and salmon. Break into large chunks; remove any bone and skin from salmon. Place in small bowl; toss with remaining dressing. Refrigerate, covered.

5. To serve: In shallow serving dish or bowl, arrange potato slices and onion rings in layers alternately with fish mixture. Sprinkle dill over top. Garnish with lettuce.

Makes 6 servings.

Palace Court Salad

Dressing

½ cup mayonnaise or cooked
salad dressing
2 tablespoons milk
2 tablespoons finely chopped
stuffed olives

1 tablespoon finely chopped
green pepper
1 tablespoon finely chopped
onion
1 tablespoon chili sauce

Salad

1 package (9 ounces) frozen
artichoke hearts
6 tablespoons bottled clear
French dressing
2 cans (7½-ounce size)
king-crab meat

2 large tomatoes
4 cups finely shredded crisp
iceberg lettuce

Ripe olives

1. Make Dressing: In small bowl, combine all dressing ingredients; mix well. Refrigerate, covered, until well chilled—2 to 3 hours.

2. Meanwhile, make Salad: Cook artichoke hearts as package label directs. Drain; turn into medium-size bowl. Toss with 3 tablespoons French dressing. Refrigerate, covered, until well chilled—about 2 hours.

3. Drain crab meat. Remove any cartilage. Toss with remaining French dressing in medium-size bowl. Refrigerate, covered, until chilled—about 2 hours.

4. Trim ends from tomatoes; discard. Halve tomatoes crosswise.

5. Place 1 cup lettuce in each of 4 individual salad bowls. Top each with a tomato half; arrange artichoke hearts on tomatoes; mound crab meat high on top. Garnish with ripe olives. Spoon dressing over each salad.

Makes 4 servings.

Salmon-Stuffed Avocados

1 package (8 ounces) soft
  cream cheese
2 cans (7½-ounce size) salmon,
  drained
2 teaspoons Worcestershire
  sauce

1½ teaspoons salt
⅛ teaspoon pepper
3 avocados, black or green skin
1 tablespoon lemon juice

1. In large bowl, with wooden spoon, beat the cream cheese with salmon, Worcestershire, salt, and pepper until fluffy.
2. Halve avocados lengthwise; remove pits. Brush cut sides with lemon juice, to prevent discoloration.
3. Fill hollow of each half with cream-cheese mixture. Refrigerate until well chilled—about 1 hour.
Makes 6 servings.

Sardine Salad Platter

1 can (3¾ ounces) smoked
  sardines
1 can (4⅜ ounces) boneless
  sardines in oil
1 can (3¾ ounces) sardines in
  tomato sauce and sherry

4 hard-cooked eggs, sliced
½ bunch fresh dill
2 medium-size ripe tomatoes

Sauce

¾ cup mayonnaise or cooked
  salad dressing
2 tablespoons prepared mustard
  with horseradish

½ teaspoon cider vinegar
⅛ teaspoon seasoned salt

1. Drain sardines. Place in separate mounds in center of large, round serving platter. Arrange egg slices, overlapping, around the sardines.
2. Surround eggs with dill. Cut each tomato into 8 wedges; arrange tomatoes on dill. Refrigerate 1 hour.
3. Just before serving, make Sauce: In small bowl, combine all sauce ingredients until thoroughly blended. Pass sauce with salad.
Makes 4 to 6 servings.

Seafood Chef's Salad

1 pound fillets of sole*
½ teaspoon salt
1 can (7½ ounces) king-crab meat, drained
1 medium-size (1½ pounds) boiled lobster or 2 (8-ounce size) cooked frozen rock-lobster tails
½ pound shrimp, cooked, shelled, and deveined
½ cup bottled Italian-style dressing

Dressing

⅓ cup chili sauce
⅔ cup mayonnaise
¼ cup chopped onion
¼ cup chopped green pepper
2 tablespoons lemon juice
⅛ teaspoon salt

2 heads Boston lettuce, washed and chilled

¼ pound Swiss cheese, cut in strips
4 hard-cooked eggs, sliced
2 medium-size tomatoes, cut in eighths

4 anchovy fillets, drained
1 tablespoon capers, drained

1. Place fillets of sole in medium-size skillet. Add cold water to cover; sprinkle with ½ teaspoon salt; bring to boiling. Reduce heat; simmer, covered, 5 minutes, or until fish flakes easily when tested with a fork.

2. Remove sole from liquid; drain. Place in shallow baking dish. Carefully remove any membrane from crab meat. Arrange lobster meat, shrimp, and crab meat in separate mounds in same dish.

3. Drizzle with Italian-style dressing. Refrigerate, covered, until well chilled—at least 3 hours.

4. Meanwhile, make Dressing: In medium-size bowl, combine all dressing ingredients. Refrigerate.

5. To serve: Line a large, chilled bowl with lettuce leaves. Arrange salad ingredients attractively: Place sole in center of bowl; shrimp at each end; crab, lobster, and cheese on each side. Arrange egg slices and tomato wedges between mounds of seafood. Garnish eggs with anchovy fillets and sole with capers. Pass dressing.

Makes 8 servings.

---

*Or use 1 cup of any cooked leftover white fish.

Tuna-Macaroni Supper Salad

1 package (8 ounces) elbow macaroni
1 cup mayonnaise or cooked salad dressing
½ cup Italian-style dressing
1 tablespoon prepared mustard
2 cups thin, pared cucumber slices
1½ cups diced tomato
½ cup diced green pepper

¼ cup coarsely chopped green onion
1 teaspoon salt
⅛ teaspoon pepper
2 cans (7-ounce size) solid-pack tuna, drained

1 hard-cooked egg, chopped
Chicory
Chopped parsley

1. Cook macaroni as package label directs. Drain; rinse with cold water.

2. In large bowl, combine mayonnaise, Italian-style dressing, and mustard; mix well.

3. Add cucumber, tomato, green pepper, green onion, salt, pepper, tuna in large pieces, and macaroni; toss to mix well. Turn into salad bowl.

4. Refrigerate, covered, until well chilled—about 4 hours.

5. Just before serving, garnish with hard-cooked egg, chicory, and parsley.

Makes 8 servings.

Calypso Fruit Salad

7 medium-size ripe bananas
1 cup dairy sour cream
¼ cup light rum
2 tablespoons brown sugar
¼ teaspoon ginger
⅛ teaspoon salt
2 teaspoons lime juice
Lettuce leaves

1 can (1 pound, 1 ounce) peach halves, drained and chilled
2 pint boxes strawberries, washed and hulled; or 2 packages (1-pound size) frozen whole strawberries, thawed and drained

1. In medium-size bowl, mash 1 banana with fork. Add sour cream, rum, sugar, ginger, salt, and lime juice; mix well. Refrigerate, covered, until well chilled—at least 1 hour.

2. Just before serving, arrange a bed of lettuce leaves on serving platter. Slice remaining 6 bananas in half lengthwise. Arrange on lettuce with peach halves and strawberries.

3. Serve with banana-rum dressing.

Makes 6 servings.

Curried-Chicken-and-Fresh-Fruit Salad

Curry Mayonnaise

½ cup mayonnaise or cooked salad dressing

1 tablespoon chopped preserved ginger in syrup

2 teaspoons curry powder

1 teaspoon grated onion

½ teaspoon salt

½ cup heavy cream, whipped

3 cups cubed cooked chicken or turkey

¼ cup bottled oil-and-vinegar dressing

2 cups fresh pineapple, in 1-inch chunks; or 1 can (1 pound, 4½ ounces) pineapple chunks, drained

1½ cups diced pared apple (1 large)

1½ cups seedless green grapes

¼ cup chutney

¼ cup chopped green pepper

Crisp lettuce

Watercress (optional)

1. Make Curry Mayonnaise: In small bowl, combine mayonnaise, ginger, curry, onion, and salt; mix until well blended. Fold in cream just until combined. Refrigerate, covered, until needed.

2. In large bowl, combine chicken and oil-and-vinegar dressing; toss until well coated. Refrigerate, covered, at least 2 hours.

3. Add pineapple, apple, grapes, chutney, and green pepper to chicken; mix well. Gently fold in curry mayonnaise until well blended.

4. Refrigerate, covered, until chilled—about 2 hours.

5. To serve: Arrange lettuce leaves on platter. Mound salad in center. If desired, garnish with watercress.

Makes 6 to 8 servings.

Fruit Salad Tropicana

Frosted Grapes

6 small clusters black grapes
1 egg white, slightly beaten
½ cup sugar

2 cups creamed cottage cheese
¼ cup finely chopped crystallized ginger
1 cup canned mandarin-orange sections, drained

Dressing

½ cup mayonnaise or cooked salad dressing
2 tablespoons milk
1 tablespoon lemon juice
½ teaspoon ground ginger
Dash salt
¼ cup liquid from pineapple spears

Crisp iceberg-lettuce leaves
9 fresh apricots, halved and pitted
12 canned pineapple spears
1 unpared red apple, cut into 12 slices

6 watercress sprigs

1. Prepare Frosted Grapes: Wash grapes; let dry. Dip grapes in egg white to coat; shake off excess; then roll in sugar. Place grapes on wire rack. Let stand at room temperature to dry.

2. Meanwhile, combine cottage cheese, crystallized ginger, and mandarin oranges in medium-size bowl; mix gently to combine. Refrigerate, covered, until ready to use.

3. Also, make Dressing: In small bowl, combine all dressing ingredients. Beat, with rotary beater, until well combined. Refrigerate, covered, until ready to use.

4. To serve: Place lettuce leaves on 6 chilled salad plates. Mound some of cottage-cheese mixture in center of each.

5. Arrange 3 apricot halves, 2 pineapple spears, 2 apple slices, and a cluster of frosted grapes around cottage cheese on each plate. Garnish with watercress sprigs.

6. Pass dressing along with salad.

Makes 6 servings.

Honeydew Salad

Dressing

1 bottle (8 ounces)
  oil-and-vinegar dressing
2 ounces blue cheese, crumbled

6 small heads Bibb lettuce
2 Belgian endives
1 pint box strawberries
1 large Spanish or honeydew
  melon

2 medium-size bananas

Lemon juice
1 can (1 pound, 1 ounce) dark,
  sweet pitted cherries
1 can (11 ounces) mandarin
  oranges

1. Make Dressing: In jar with tight-fitting lid, combine dressing and cheese; shake vigorously. Refrigerate until chilled—several hours.

2. Wash lettuce; drain well on paper towels. Wash endives, and separate leaves. Wash strawberries, but do not hull. Make 2 cups large melon balls. Peel bananas; cut into ½-inch-thick slices. Dip in lemon juice. Refrigerate greens, prepared fruit, and canned fruit until chilled—several hours.

3. To serve: Drain canned fruit well. Place a head of lettuce on each of 6 chilled salad plates. Remove center leaves from each head, and arrange on plate around head. Mound melon balls in center of lettuce heads. Arrange strawberries, banana slices, cherries, and orange sections, in separate groups, in and around melon balls. Garnish with endive leaves.

4. Shake dressing vigorously, and pass separately.

Makes 6 servings.

Panorama Fruit Plate

Horseradish Dressing

½ cup salad oil
¼ cup lemon juice
2 tablespoons sugar
1¼ teaspoons celery seed

1 teaspoon prepared
  horseradish
¾ teaspoon seasoned salt

Salad

2 fresh pears, pared, cored, and
   sliced
3 bananas, cut into 1-inch
   pieces
1 green- or black-skin avocado,
   peeled and sliced
¼ cup lemon juice

3 cups cantaloupe balls
3 cups watermelon chunks
1 can (1 pound, 1 ounce) pitted
   Bing cherries

12 crisp Boston-lettuce leaves
Preserved kumquats or ginger

1. Make Horseradish Dressing: In small bowl, combine oil with rest of dressing ingredients; beat, with rotary beater, to mix well. Pour into a jar with a tight-fitting lid. Refrigerate until ready to use.

2. Make Salad: Prepare fruit. Dip pears, bananas, and avocado in lemon juice. Refrigerate all fruit, covered, until ready to use.

3. To serve: Arrange lettuce on 6 chilled salad plates. Drain cherries. Mound each kind of fruit separately on lettuce. Garnish each plate with a few kumquats.

4. Serve with dressing (shake well before using), along with hot rolls, if desired.

Makes 6 servings.

Rainbow Salad Plate

Dressing

½ cup salad oil
¼ cup lemon juice
1 tablespoon sugar
1 tablespoon white vinegar
2 teaspoons grated lemon peel
½ teaspoon salt

6 nectarines
2 tablespoons lemon juice
1 package (3 ounces) soft
   cream cheese
⅓ cup grated sharp Cheddar
   cheese

2 tablespoons dry sherry
12 pecan halves
1 medium-size honeydew
   melon
1 pint lemon sherbet
1 package (10 ounces) frozen
   raspberries, thawed and
   drained
6 small grape clusters

Watercress sprigs

Hot, buttered muffins (optional)

1. Make Dressing: Combine all dressing ingredients in jar with tight-fitting lid; shake vigorously to combine. Refrigerate until ready to use.

2. Peel nectarines; halve; remove pits. Dip nectarines in 2 tablespoons lemon juice.

3. In small bowl, combine cream cheese, Cheddar cheese, and sherry; mix until well combined. Use mixture to fill hollows in nectarines.

4. Top each with a pecan half; refrigerate until ready to use.

5. To serve: Cut a slice off each end of melon, and discard. Then cut melon crosswise into 6 slices. Remove rind and seeds.

6. Arrange melon rings on 6 chilled salad plates. Place a scoop of sherbet in center of each; spoon raspberries over top.

7. Arrange 2 nectarine halves and a grape cluster around sherbet on each ring. Garnish with watercress.

8. Serve with dressing (shake well before using) and hot, buttered muffins, if desired.

Makes 6 servings.

Sunnyside Fruit Salad Plate

1 cup diced avocado	1 cup sliced strawberries
5 plums, quartered	2 tablespoons sliced toasted almonds
3 tablespoons lime juice	
¼ cup bottled clear French dressing	
2 cups cantaloupe balls, chilled	
1 package (13½ ounces) frozen pineapple chunks, thawed and drained	
12 crisp Boston-lettuce leaves	

1. Sprinkle avocado and plums with half of the lime juice. Refrigerate both fruits, covered, until ready to use.

2. Combine French dressing with rest of lime juice; mix well.

3. Just before serving, combine avocado, plums, melon balls, pineapple chunks, and dressing. Toss gently to combine.

4. Arrange lettuce leaves on 6 chilled salad plates, to form cups. Then fill lettuce cups with fruit mixture.

5. Garnish top of each salad with sliced strawberries and toasted almonds.

Makes 6 servings.

Summer Salad Plate with Blue-Cheese Dressing

Blue-Cheese Dressing

½ cup mayonnaise or cooked salad dressing
¼ cup bottled herb dressing
½ cup crumbled blue cheese
2 tablespoons milk
2 tablespoons lemon juice

3 fresh pears
2 tablespoons lemon juice
3 navel oranges
1 pint box blueberries
12 large strawberries, unhulled
4 cups honeydew-melon balls
Crisp iceberg-lettuce leaves

1. Make Blue-Cheese Dressing: In small bowl, combine mayonnaise, herb dressing, blue cheese, milk, and 2 tablespoons lemon juice. Beat, with rotary beater, until well combined.

2. Refrigerate dressing, covered, until ready to use.

3. Pare pears; halve; core. Dip pears in 2 tablespoons lemon juice. Peel oranges, removing any white membrane; cut each orange crosswise into 6 slices. Wash blueberries and strawberries; drain. Refrigerate all fruit until ready to use.

4. To serve: Arrange lettuce leaves on 6 chilled salad plates. Place pear halves, cut side up, on lettuce; spoon blueberries over pears.

5. Arrange 3 orange slices and ⅔ cup melon balls around pear on each plate. Garnish with 2 strawberries.

6. Serve dressing over salad, and pass hot, buttered muffins, if desired.

Makes 6 servings.

Tossed Fruit Salad

1 small head Boston or Bibb lettuce
½ head romaine
8 watercress sprigs
4 plums
4 fresh peaches; or 1 package (12 ounces) frozen sliced peaches, thawed and drained

1 banana
⅓ cup lemon juice
1 pint fresh strawberries, washed and hulled
Roquefort Dressing (see p. 107)
6 small clusters seedless green grapes

1. Wash lettuce, romaine, and watercress; dry well. Store in crisper until ready to use.

2. Refrigerate rest of ingredients until ready to use.

3. Line shallow salad bowl with crisp, chilled outer lettuce leaves. Break rest of greens into bite-size pieces to measure 3 cups. Turn into a bowl.

4. Just before serving, prepare fruit: Cut plums into 8 sections. Peel peaches; cut into 8 sections. Peel banana; with tines of fork, flute lengthwise; cut into ¾-inch diagonal pieces. Sprinkle plums, peaches, and banana with lemon juice, to keep fruit from darkening. Reserve 6 strawberries for garnish; cut rest in half.

5. To serve: Add prepared fruit to greens. Toss with Roquefort Dressing until well coated. Turn into lettuce-lined bowl.

6. Garnish with watercress sprigs, reserved whole strawberries, and the grape clusters.

Makes 4 servings.

Roquefort Dressing

½ cup salad oil
2 tablespoons white-wine vinegar
2 tablespoons lemon juice
½ teaspoon salt
½ teaspoon celery seed

⅛ teaspoon pepper
½ teaspoon sugar
½ teaspoon paprika
⅓ cup crumbled Roquefort cheese

1. Combine all ingredients in jar with tight-fitting lid. Shake vigorously to combine.

2. Refrigerate until ready to use. Shake dressing again before using. Makes about 1 cup.

Molded Salads

Ham-and-Potato-Salad Mold

2 packages (6-ounce size) sliced boiled ham
2 cans (1-pound size) whole potatoes
1 cup finely chopped celery
¼ cup chopped parsley
2 hard-cooked eggs, chopped
1 pimiento, chopped

2 tablespoons sweet-pickle relish, drained
1 tablespoon instant minced onion
1 teaspoon salt
¼ teaspoon pepper
1 envelope unflavored gelatin
1 cup mayonnaise or cooked salad dressing

1. Line a 9- by 5- by 3-inch loaf pan with foil, letting foil extend over sides. Line bottom and sides with ham from one package.

2. Cut remaining ham into ½-inch squares. Rinse potatoes with cold water; drain. Cut into ½-inch cubes.

3. In large bowl, combine ham squares, potato, celery, parsley, egg, pimiento, pickle relish, minced onion, salt, and pepper.

4. In small saucepan, sprinkle gelatin over ½ cup water to soften. Place over low heat, and stir until gelatin is dissolved. Remove from heat; stir in mayonnaise until smooth. Add to potato mixture; toss until well blended. Turn into ham-lined pan, pressing down firmly.

5. Place in freezer 40 minutes, to chill quickly.

6. To unmold: Lift foil to loosen loaf; invert onto serving plate. Peel off foil.

Makes 8 servings.

Note: Refrigerate, covered, until firm—at least 4 hours—if you can allow more time.

Perfection Salad

3 envelopes unflavored gelatin
½ cup sugar

½ teaspoon salt
½ teaspoon seasoned salt

4 cups boiling water
1 beef-bouillon cube, dissolved
   in ½ cup boiling water
½ cup tarragon vinegar
3 tablespoons lemon juice
⅛ teaspoon Tabasco
1 cup coarsely chopped pared
   carrot

½ cup coarsely chopped green
   pepper
½ cup finely chopped celery
½ cup sweet-pickle relish,
   drained
2 pimientos, drained and cut up
6 lettuce cups

Celery-Seed Dressing (see below)

1. In large bowl, combine gelatin, sugar, and salts, mixing well. Add boiling water, stirring until gelatin mixture is dissolved.

2. Stir in bouillon, vinegar, lemon juice, and Tabasco; refrigerate until mixture is consistency of unbeaten egg white.

3. Fold in rest of ingredients, except lettuce, combining well. Turn into 10- by 6- by 2-inch pan; refrigerate until firm—several hours, or overnight.

4. To serve: Cut into 6 pieces; place each on lettuce cup on salad plate. Serve with Celery-Seed Dressing.

Makes 6 servings.

Celery-Seed Dressing

2 tablespoons lemon juice
1 cup mayonnaise or cooked
   salad dressing
1 teaspoon celery seed

1. Blend lemon juice into mayonnaise until well mixed.
2. Stir in celery seed.

Makes about 1 cup—enough for 6 servings.

Molded Crab-Meat Salad

2 envelopes unflavored gelatin
2 tablespoons dry sherry
½ cup hot canned chicken broth
2 egg yolks

1 can (7½ ounces) king-crab
   meat, drained, cartilage
   removed, flaked
5 drops Tabasco

½ cup mayonnaise or cooked
   salad dressing
1 stalk celery, coarsely cut
1 medium-size onion slice, ¼
   inch thick
1 tablespoon parsley

¼ teaspoon dried marjoram
   leaves
1 cup cream or milk
2 egg whites, stiffly beaten

Fish Dressing (see below)

1. Place gelatin, sherry, and broth in blender container; blend at high speed, covered, 40 seconds.
2. Add egg yolks, crab meat, Tabasco, mayonnaise, celery, onion, parsley, and marjoram. Blend at high speed, covered, about 15 seconds, stopping once to stir.
3. Remove cover. With motor on, pour in cream.
4. Fold mixture into egg whites.
5. Pour into 1-quart mold, and refrigerate until firm—about 1 hour.
6. Unmold, and serve with Fish Dressing.
Makes 6 servings.

Fish Dressing

¼ cup salad oil
½ cup spinach leaves, stems
   removed
½ cup parsley

1 clove garlic, chopped
2 tablespoons chopped chives
1¼ cups mayonnaise or cooked
   salad dressing

1. Place oil, spinach, parsley, garlic, and chives in blender container.
2. Blend at high speed, covered, turning motor on and off, until vegetables are chopped fine—about 1 minute. Stop once to stir.
3. Place mayonnaise in bowl. Fold in chopped vegetables.
4. Serve with Molded Crab-Meat Salad.
Makes 1½ cups.

Pineapple-and-Cottage-Cheese Salad Ring

1 can (1 pint, 2 ounces)
   pineapple juice
⅓ cup mayonnaise or cooked
   salad dressing

1 can (1 pound, 4½ ounces)
   crushed pineapple
2 envelopes unflavored gelatin
¼ cup lemon juice

¼ cup sugar
⅛ teaspoon salt
Few drops yellow food coloring
1 cup finely chopped celery

1 cup creamed cottage cheese

Crisp salad greens

1. Mix ¼ cup pineapple juice with the mayonnaise. Refrigerate, covered, until needed. Pour remaining juice into 1-quart measure; add syrup drained from crushed pineapple and, if necessary, water to make 3 cups liquid.

2. In medium-size saucepan, sprinkle gelatin over 1 cup pineapple liquid to soften. Then place over low heat, stirring constantly, until gelatin is dissolved. Remove gelatin mixture from heat; add remaining pineapple liquid, the lemon juice, sugar, salt, and yellow food coloring, stirring until the sugar is dissolved.

3. Turn into bowl. Refrigerate until mixture is consistency of unbeaten egg white—about 1 hour.

4. Fold in crushed pineapple, celery, and cottage cheese. Turn into 1½-quart ring mold that has been rinsed in cold water.

5. Refrigerate until firm enough to unmold—several hours or overnight.

6. To serve: Run a small spatula around edge of mold. Invert over platter; place a hot, damp dishcloth over inverted mold, and shake gently to release. Garnish with salad greens. Place mayonnaise mixture in cup in center of mold.

Makes 4 to 6 servings.

Molded Fruit-and-Cottage-Cheese Salad

1 can (1 pound, 1 ounce) pear halves
1 can (8¾ ounces) apricot halves

1 can (8¾ ounces) light seedless grapes

Fruit Layer

¾ cup boiling water
1 package (3 ounces) pink-grapefruit-flavored gelatin

¾ cup syrup from fruits

Cottage-Cheese Layer
¾ cup boiling water
1 package (3 ounces)
  pink-grapefruit-flavored
  gelatin

½ cup syrup from fruits
1 cup small-curd creamed
  cottage cheese

Dressing
⅓ cup mayonnaise or cooked
  salad dressing
⅓ cup dairy sour cream

2 tablespoons apricot preserves

Salad greens

1. Drain fruits, reserving the syrups. Mix syrups; reserve 1¼ cups.
2. Make Fruit Layer: In medium-size bowl, pour ¾ cup boiling water over gelatin; stir to dissolve gelatin. Stir in ¾ cup syrup from fruits.
3. Pour ¾ cup gelatin mixture into a 4½-cup ring mold. Refrigerate until firm—15 minutes.
4. Fill centers of 6 pear halves and 4 apricot halves with some of grapes. Arrange pears and apricots, alternately and cut side down, over gelatin in ring mold.
5. Pour remaining gelatin mixture over fruit. Refrigerate until firm.
6. Meanwhile, make Cottage-Cheese Layer: In medium-size bowl, pour ¾ cup boiling water over gelatin; stir to dissolve gelatin.
7. Add ½ cup reserved syrup from fruits, and cottage cheese; mix well. Refrigerate until mixture is consistency of unbeaten egg white—about 45 minutes.
8. Cut remaining pears and apricots in quarters. Fold into cheese-gelatin mixture, along with rest of grapes. Spoon over fruit layer, spreading evenly. Refrigerate until firm—several hours, or overnight.
9. Just before serving, make Dressing: In small bowl, with rotary beater, beat mayonnaise, sour cream, and preserves until combined.
10. To unmold salad: Run a spatula around edge of mold; invert over serving platter; shake gently to release. If necessary, place a hot, damp cloth over mold; shake again to release. Surround with salad greens. Pass dressing.

Makes 4 to 6 servings.

Ginger-and-Fresh-Fruit Salad Mold

1 cup boiling water	1 pint strawberries
2 packages (3-ounce size) or 1 package (6 ounces) orange-flavored gelatin	¼ pound seedless green grapes
	1 cup cantaloupe balls
	1 cup honeydew balls
3 bottles (7-ounce size) or 2½ cups ginger ale	
	Ginger Dressing (see below)

1. In large bowl, pour boiling water over gelatin; stir until gelatin is dissolved. Stir in ginger ale.

2. Refrigerate, stirring occasionally, until mixture is consistency of unbeaten egg white—about 1 hour.

3. Meanwhile, wash strawberries. Hull and halve enough to make 1 cup. Set aside the rest for garnish. Wash and drain grapes, to use for garnish.

4. Fold melon balls and halved strawberries into thickened gelatin. Carefully turn mixture into a decorative 6-cup mold.

5. Refrigerate until firm—at least 4 hours.

6. To unmold: Run a small spatula around edge of mold. Invert onto serving plate. Place a hot dishcloth over mold; shake gently to release. Repeat, if necessary. Lift off mold.

7. Refrigerate until ready to serve. Garnish with grapes and reserved strawberries. Serve with Ginger Dressing.

Makes 4 to 6 servings.

Ginger Dressing

½ cup heavy cream	1 tablespoon chopped preserved ginger in syrup
¼ cup mayonnaise or cooked salad dressing	1 tablespoon syrup from ginger

1. In small bowl, whip cream until stiff. Fold in mayonnaise, ginger, and syrup.

2. Refrigerate until serving time.

Makes 1⅓ cups.

Cheese and Fresh-Fruit Plates

Gelatin Rings

1 cup boiling water	1 package (3 ounces) pink-grapefruit-flavored gelatin

½ cup pecan halves

¾ cup thinly sliced peeled fresh peaches

Cream-Cheese Balls

2 packages (3-ounce size) soft cream cheese

1 jar (4 ounces) diced candied fruits and peels, finely chopped

Dressing

½ cup dairy sour cream
¼ cup honey
2 tablespoons lemon juice
½ teaspon salt
¼ teaspoon dry mustard

1 can (13¼ ounces) pineapple chunks, drained
2 cups fresh-grapefruit sections
1 cup blue-plum slices

Crisp Boston-lettuce leaves

1. Make Gelatin Rings: In medium-size bowl, pour boiling water over gelatin; stir to dissolve gelatin. Add ¾ cup cold water.
2. Pour 2 tablespoons gelatin mixture into each of 6 (4-ounce size) individual ring molds. Refrigerate, uncovered, 10 to 15 minutes, or until gelatin is consistency of unbeaten egg white.
3. Arrange pecan halves, then peach slices, in single rows, over thickened gelatin in each mold. Then pour rest of gelatin into molds. Refrigerate, uncovered, until firm—about 2 hours.
4. Meanwhile, make Cream-Cheese Balls: Divide each package of cream cheese into 3 parts. Form each part into a ball. Roll balls in candied-fruit mixture to coat. Refrigerate, uncovered.
5. Make Dressing: Combine all dressing ingredients in small bowl. Beat, with rotary beater, until well combined. Refrigerate, covered.
6. To serve: Arrange lettuce leaves on 6 chilled salad plates.
7. Run a small spatula around edges of each ring mold. Dip bottom of each mold in warm water a few seconds; invert on lettuce leaves.
8. Arrange the pineapple chunks, grapefruit sections, and plum slices around gelatin rings. Add a cream-cheese ball to each plate.
9. Serve with dressing (beat again just before serving) and hot, buttered English muffins, if desired.
Makes 6 servings.

IV

Savory Stews and Rewarding Ragouts

❀ ❀ ❀

People are forever asking the cook, "What is in this sauce?" or "How many egg whites go in an angel cake?" or "Is it red or white wine you add to a beef bourguignon?" Those are the times when instead of a chef's hat and a collection of recipes, a cook's insignia should be a mortar board and an encyclopedia.

Perhaps the most exasperating culinary question is the one that asks the difference between a stew and a ragout. Personally, I am convinced this must have been one of the riddles posed by the ancient Sphinx of Thebes. It's one of those queries no two cooks answer the same way.

Ragout, from the French verb *ragoûter,* meaning to revive the taste, is, by definition, a stew made from regular-size pieces of meat, fish, or poultry. Most often the term is applied to well-seasoned meat and vegetables cooked in a thick sauce.

The truth is that a ragout can be a stew but a stew isn't necessarily a ragout. To get technical again, stewing is "a method of cooking food in liquid by simmering, or long, slow cooking just below boiling point in a pan or casserole with a tightly-fitting lid." Usually, a stew is a meat or

115

fish dish with vegetables; however, *any* food prepared by slow simmering heat can be considered a stew.

But enough of definitions. Stews and ragouts, at their best, are beyond description. Gourmets and gourmands love them; homemakers recognize their versatility. They are delightfully economical, and their humble origins needn't show. No one has to know the cook bought an inexpensive cut of meat and cubed it herself. And that long simmering cooking process produces a marvelous aroma that seeps through the house, making noses twitch and taste buds flower, so that even the most nonchalant diner will ask anxiously, "How soon will dinner be ready?"

Furthermore, stews and ragouts do not require constant attention. While they simmer away on the stove, you can keep busy elsewhere. Both are dishes with admirable staying power. Unlike other main courses that demand immediate serving to be at their best, stews and ragouts will sit on the back of the stove and wait and wait and wait. And taste just as good when served to the latecomer who arrives at nine o'clock instead of seven, explaining that somehow he got on the express thruway and couldn't get off. (It really wouldn't matter if he didn't find his way home until the next day—stews taste even better then.) And if a guest unexpectedly brings a friend or two with him, that is no calamity, either. Stews are eminently stretchable. You can thin the gravy. You can add a can of drained small potatoes or tomatoes. You can top a hot, bubbling stew with a snowy crust of dumplings. Presto— what was intended for six will now feed eight.

Stews and ragouts are classified by color; they are either white or brown. A white stew is easier to put together than a brown one, but both call for the same slow, gentle cooking. Anything approaching a boil will toughen the meat and cause too much reduction of the gravy. (Old-time cooks had their own way of describing the simmering process: they said it happens "when the broth smiles.")

White stews, sometimes labeled fricassees or blanquettes, are made with "white" meat, such as lamb, chicken, or veal. Brown stews are those in which the pieces of meat are browned quickly on all sides, to seal in the flavor. This searing process gives the meat an agreeable color, coloring the liquid as well. Don't overdo the browning since the meat will become dry and tasteless. Cut the meat into about one- or two-inch squares. Since meat shrinks during the cooking, anything smaller won't look substantial. Vegetables should also be cut neatly in fair-sized pieces, with the small vegetables, like baby carrots, used whole. The proper temperature for stewing is between 135° and 160° F. Make sure your stew kettle is tightly covered. If the lid fits badly, put a piece of foil across the top of the pan beneath the cover. Before thickening or serving the stew, skim off any excess fat on the surface; in that way, you'll get its true flavor.

We must not ignore one of the most famous of all stews—goulash—of which there are some examples in this chapter. Generally made with beef and, occasionally, veal, a goulash is always highly seasoned and contains paprika and a large proportion of onion.

Another intriguing stew is the famous West Coast specialty Cioppino. A first cousin of the bouillabaisse of Mediterranean countries, Cioppino (pronounced cho-peen-o) is a fisherman's chowder created years ago by fishermen who chugged in and out of San Francisco harbor in their fishing boats, using the day's catch to make a hearty meal. In fact, this unusual stew has been known to contain as many as a dozen different kinds of fish.

Can stews and ragouts be made in advance and frozen for future use? But of course. For best results, you'll want to observe these few rules. Be careful not to overcook a stew that you plan to freeze; otherwise, when it is reheated it will be "cooked out" and have a limp, flavorless taste. Always cool promptly by submerging the saucepan or kettle in which it has cooked in a large pan of ice and water. Skim off the fat that rises to the surface. Be sure to leave headspace in the freezer container. Incidentally, if your recipe calls for garlic, omit it from the stew to be frozen—garlic becomes stronger during storage. Potatoes do not freeze well either; add them when you thaw your stew. Onions gradually lose their flavor under freezing conditions, so do not keep a frozen stew with onions in the freezer more than three or four months.

When you are ready to serve the frozen stew, partially thaw it at room temperature. Then heat in a double boiler for 30 to 40 minutes, adding more liquid if necessary. Don't overstir, in order not to destroy the shape and appearance of the vegetables.

If you have cooked your ragout or stew in an attractive casserole or pot, bring it right to the table as is. Stews are like fashionable women— they can be dressed up or down, depending on the occasion, and look perfectly right. Whether you spoon it out from the cooking dish or transfer it first to an antique silver serving dish, you'll never have to apologize for a stew's appearance.

It may amuse you to know that stew pots have enjoyed tremendous status down through the centuries. Achilles thought so highly of a caldron in which stew had been cooked that he offered it to the winner of an important chariot race. The caldron happened to have been embossed in gold and have silver handles, but the Greek warrior didn't care about its elaborate workmanship. What he bragged about was the fact that when the caldron was filled with stew, it held seventeen gallons!

Browned Beef-Brisket Stew

1 (3¼-pound size) fresh beef brisket	4 medium-size potatoes, pared and quartered
1 large onion, quartered	6 small carrots, pared and halved crosswise
1 cup chopped celery	
2 teaspoons salt	1 package (10 ounces) frozen peas, unthawed
¼ teaspoon pepper	
2 bay leaves	⅓ cup unsifted all-purpose flour

1. Wipe brisket with damp paper towels. Slowly heat large Dutch oven. Add brisket, fat side down; brown slowly, turning—about 15 minutes in all.

2. Add onion, celery, salt, pepper, bay leaves, and 1 quart water; bring to boiling. Reduce heat; simmer, covered, 2½ hours, or until almost fork-tender.

3. Add potatoes, carrots, and peas; simmer, covered, at least 30 minutes, or until beef and vegetables are tender.

4. Meanwhile, in small bowl, combine flour and ½ cup water, stirring until smooth. Stir into liquid in Dutch oven; bring to boiling. Reduce heat; simmer, uncovered, 5 minutes.

5. Serve brisket with gravy and vegetables.

Makes 4 to 6 servings.

Beef-and-Vegetable Stew

3   pounds stew beef
6   tablespoons salad oil
1   cup chopped onion
1   cup chopped green pepper
1   cup sliced celery
1   can (10½ ounces) condensed beef broth, undiluted
1   can (8 ounces) tomato sauce
2   tablespoons chopped parsley
1   clove garlic, finely chopped
1   tablespoon salt
¼   teaspoon pepper
⅛   teaspoon dried thyme leaves
1   bay leaf
6   small potatoes, pared and halved (about 2 pounds)
6   medium-size carrots, pared (about ¾ pound)
6   small white onions, peeled
1   to 2 tablespoons flour
1   tomato, cut in wedges (optional)

1. Cut beef into 1-inch pieces. In hot oil in Dutch oven, over medium heat, brown one-third meat at a time (just enough to cover bottom of pan) until browned on all sides. Remove as browned.

2. Add chopped onion, green pepper, and celery to Dutch oven, and sauté until tender—about 8 minutes. Return beef to pan.

3. Add ½ cup water, the beef broth, tomato sauce, parsley, garlic, salt, pepper, thyme, and bay leaf; bring to boiling. Reduce heat; simmer, covered and stirring several times, 1¼ hours.

4. Add potatoes, carrots, and onions. Simmer, covered, 1 hour longer, or until meat and vegetables are tender. Remove from heat; skim off fat.

5. Mix flour with 2 tablespoons water. Stir into beef mixture. Arrange tomato wedges, skin side up, on top; simmer, covered, 10 minutes.

Makes 6 servings.

Hearty Beef Stew with Noodles

1½   tablespoons butter or margarine
1½   tablespoons salad oil
3   pounds beef chuck, cut in 1½-inch cubes
1½   cups sliced onion

4 teaspoons salt	1½ packages (8-ounce size) wide
¼ teaspoon pepper	noodles
3 teaspoons caraway seed	¾ cup coarsely crushed
2 bay leaves	gingersnaps
⅓ cup vinegar	

1. Heat butter and salad oil in 4-quart Dutch oven over medium heat. Add beef, half at a time, and brown well on all sides. Remove beef as it browns, and set aside.

2. In drippings, sauté onion until tender—about 3 minutes. Stir in 4½ cups hot water, salt, pepper, caraway seed, bay leaves, and browned meat; bring to boiling. Reduce heat; simmer, covered, 1½ hours. Add vinegar; simmer ½ hour longer.

3. Meanwhile, cook noodles as package label directs; drain. Place in heated serving dish.

4. In small bowl, combine gingersnaps with ⅓ cup cold water.

5. With slotted spoon, remove meat from Dutch oven, and arrange over noodles. Strain pan liquid. Measure 2 cups, and return to pan. Stir in gingersnaps; bring to boiling. Reduce heat; simmer 3 minutes. Pour over meat and noodles.

Makes 6 servings.

Beef Stew Carbonnade

¼ cup unsifted all-purpose flour	1 tablespoon bottled steak
2½ teaspoons salt	sauce
½ teaspoon pepper	2 bay leaves
2 pounds beef chuck, cut in	½ teaspoon dried thyme leaves
1-inch cubes	2 pounds potatoes, pared and
½ cup salad oil	quartered
2 pounds onions, peeled and	1 package (10 ounces) frozen
sliced	peas
1 clove garlic, crushed	
1 can (12 ounces) light beer	2 tablespoons chopped parsley
1 tablespoon soy sauce	
1 tablespoon Worcestershire	
sauce	

1. Combine flour, salt, and pepper; use to coat chuck well.

2. In ¼ cup hot oil in 4-quart Dutch oven or kettle, sauté onion and garlic until onion is tender—8 to 10 minutes. Remove, and set aside.

3. Heat remaining oil in Dutch oven. Add chuck, and brown well on all sides.

4. Add onion and garlic to Dutch oven along with beer, soy sauce, Worcestershire, steak sauce, bay leaves, and thyme; mix well.

5. Bring mixture to boiling. Reduce heat; simmer, covered, 1½ hours.

6. Add potatoes; simmer, covered, 20 minutes longer, or until potatoes are tender.

7. Add peas; simmer, covered, 8 minutes longer, or just until tender.

8. To serve: Turn stew into serving dish. Garnish with the chopped parsley.

Makes 6 servings.

Family Stew

¼ cup unsifted all-purpose flour	1 cup chopped onion
Salt	1 clove garlic, finely chopped
⅛ teaspoon pepper	1 pound carrots, pared and cut
2 pounds beef chuck, cut in	in 2-inch pieces
2-inch cubes	1 pound fresh mushrooms,
¼ cup salad oil	washed
1 tablespoon sugar	1 can (1 pound) white
1 bay leaf, crumbled	potatoes, drained
2 tablespoons lemon juice	1 can (1 pound) onions,
¼ teaspoon ground cloves	drained
½ teaspoon paprika	1 cup dry red wine
½ teaspoon Worcestershire	2 tablespoons flour
sauce	1 package (11 ounces) piecrust
¾ teaspoon liquid gravy	mix
seasoning	1 egg

1. On sheet of waxed paper, combine ¼ cup flour, ½ teaspoon salt, and the pepper. Roll beef cubes in flour mixture, to coat evenly.

2. In 6-quart Dutch oven, heat oil until very hot. Brown beef cubes over high heat, turning to brown evenly. Brown only enough at one time to cover bottom of pan. Remove beef as it browns. When all is browned, remove Dutch oven from heat, and drain off fat.

3. Return beef to Dutch oven. Add 2 cups water to meat, along with 1 tablespoon salt, the sugar, bay leaf, lemon juice, cloves, paprika, Worcestershire, gravy seasoning, chopped onion, and garlic; mix well. Over medium heat, bring to boiling, stirring occasionally.

4. Reduce heat; simmer, covered, 2 hours Add carrots; cook, covered, about 20 minutes, or until carrots are ten ler. Add mushrooms, potatoes, and onions; cook 10 minutes longer. Remove from heat.

5. Add wine to meat-and-vegetable mixture. Mix flour smoothly with ¼ cup water; stir into meat mixture. Cook over medium heat, stirring, until mixture comes to boiling. Remove from heat.

6. Using large spoon, gently transfer stew to 2½-quart casserole. Preheat oven to 400° F.

7. Meanwhile, make piecrust (for 2-crust pie) as package label directs. Roll out on lightly floured pastry cloth to fit top of casserole, allowing 1 inch extra all around, for overhang.

8. Place crust on casserole over stew, fold in pastry edge, and flute. Cut out three mushroom shapes from remaining pastry, and arrange on pastry. Cut several vents for steam with sharp knife.

9. Mix egg with 1 tablespoon water, and use to brush pastry.

10. Bake 15 to 20 minutes, or until crust is golden brown and stew is bubbly.

Makes 6 to 8 servings.

Lamb Stew with Dill

2½ pounds boneless lamb	6 new potatoes
2 tablespoons salad oil	¼ cup flour
12 small white onions, peeled	1 package (10 ounces) frozen
¾ cup tomato juice	peas
2 teaspoons salt	
¼ teaspoon pepper	Fresh dill sprig
6 medium-size carrots	

1. Cut lamb in 1-inch pieces; trim off fat. In hot oil in 4-quart Dutch oven, over medium heat, brown one-third of meat at a time until browned on all sides. Remove as browned.

2. Add onions, and brown on all sides. Remove; set aside. Pour all fat from pan.

3. Return lamb to pan. Add 2 cups water, the tomato juice, salt, and pepper; bring to boiling. Reduce heat; simmer, covered, 30 minutes.

4. Meanwhile, scrape carrots, and cut in half. Pare a band of skin, about ½ inch wide, around center of each potato.

5. Add onions, carrots, and potatoes to lamb mixture. Simmer, covered, 40 minutes longer, or until meat and vegetables are tender. Remove from heat; skim off fat.

6. Mix flour with 6 tablespoons water. Stir into lamb mixture. Add peas and 3 tablespoons snipped dill. Simmer, covered, 10 to 15 minutes longer, or until peas are tender.

7. Remove from heat; let stand 5 minutes; skim off any fat. Ladle stew into heated serving dish. Garnish with a fresh dill sprig.

Makes 6 servings.

Savory Veal Stew

6 tablespoons flour	2 chicken-bouillon cubes
2 teaspoons salt	1 cup dairy sour cream
¼ teaspoon pepper	½ cup sauterne
2 pounds veal shoulder, cut in 1½-inch cubes	1 teaspoon Worcestershire sauce
6 tablespoons butter or margarine	1½ cups sliced carrots (4 medium-size)
¾ cup chopped onion	1 package (10 ounces) frozen peas
¼ cup chopped parsley	
½ pound fresh mushrooms, washed and sliced	

1. On waxed paper, combine flour, salt, and pepper. Use some of flour mixture to coat veal cubes. Reserve remaining mixture.

2. In hot butter in 4-quart Dutch oven, brown veal. Remove as it browns.

3. Add onion, parsley, and mushrooms to drippings in Dutch oven; sauté until onion is golden—about 5 minutes. Remove from heat.

4. Stir in reserved flour mixture, stirring until well blended. Gradually stir in 2 cups water. Add bouillon cubes; bring to boiling, stirring. Stir in sour cream, sauterne, and Worcestershire; add browned veal.

5. Simmer, covered, 1 hour. Add carrots; cook, covered, 30 minutes. Then add peas, and cook, covered, 15 minutes longer.
Makes 6 servings.

Veal Stew with Sausage

1½ pounds veal shoulder, cut in 1-inch cubes
3 tablespoons flour
3 tablespoons salad oil
1 link of Italian hot sausage, cut in ½-inch-thick slices
12 small white onions, peeled (¾ pound)
1 teaspoon salt

1 envelope (1½ ounces) spaghetti-sauce mix with mushrooms
1 can (8 ounces) tomato sauce
6 medium-size carrots (¾ pound)
3 medium-size zucchini, sliced ¼ inch thick

1. Coat veal with flour. In hot oil in 4-quart Dutch oven, quickly brown veal; remove as browned.
2. Add sausage and onions to pan drippings, and sauté until golden brown. Return the browned veal to Dutch oven.
3. Stir in salt, spaghetti-sauce mix, 2 cups water, and the tomato sauce until well blended; bring to boiling. Reduce heat, and simmer, covered, 1 hour.
4. Pare carrots; cut in half lengthwise; then cut crosswise into 3-inch pieces. Add to veal mixture; simmer 45 minutes. Add zucchini, and simmer 45 minutes longer, or until meat and vegetables are tender.
Makes 6 servings.

Cioppino (Fish Stew)

⅓ cup olive or salad oil
1 cup chopped onion
1 cup chopped green onion
1 cup chopped green pepper
3 cloves garlic, crushed
1 dozen fresh littleneck clams, or 1 can (10 ounces) whole clams

1 can (1 pound, 12 ounces) tomatoes
1 can (8 ounces) tomato sauce
1 cup dry red wine
¼ cup chopped parsley
2 teaspoons salt
½ teaspoon dried oregano leaves
¼ teaspoon dried basil leaves

¼ teaspoon pepper
1 pound fresh cod
¾ pound fresh red snapper or
    striped bass

1 package (8 ounces) frozen
    rock-lobster tails

Hot Italian bread (optional)

1. In hot oil in 6-quart kettle or Dutch oven, sauté onion, green onion, green pepper, and garlic, stirring occasionally, until onion is golden—about 10 minutes.

2. Open clams, reserving liquid; set clams aside. (If you are using canned clams, drain, reserving the liquid.)

3. Add clam liquid, tomatoes, tomato sauce, wine, parsley, salt, oregano, basil, pepper, and 1 cup water to the sautéed vegetables; mix well.

4. Bring to boiling; reduce heat; simmer, covered, 30 minutes.

5. Meanwhile, rinse cod, red snapper, and lobster tails under cold water; drain. Cut cod and snapper in large pieces.

6. Add fish, unthawed lobster tails in shell, and clams to vegetable mixture. Return just to boiling; reduce heat, and simmer, covered, 30 minutes.

7. Serve with hot, crusty Italian bread, if desired.

Makes 8 servings.

Creamy Oyster Stew

3 dozen oysters on the half
    shell*
¼ cup butter or margarine
¼ cup chopped leeks
1½ teaspoons salt
½ teaspoon celery salt
¼ teaspoon white pepper
3 cups light cream

2 cups milk
⅔ cup white wine

Paprika
Chopped parsley

Oyster crackers

1. Remove the oysters from half shell; set aside.

2. In hot butter in 4-quart saucepan, sauté leeks 5 minutes.

*Or use 3 cans (7-ounce size) frozen oysters. Thaw; drain; reserve ¼ cup liquid. Then proceed as above.

3. Add oysters and any oyster liquid, the salts, and pepper; bring to boiling.

4. Heat cream and milk; add to oysters with wine. Heat, but do not boil.

5. Sprinkle with paprika and chopped parsley. Pass crackers.
Makes 8 servings.

Beef Ragout

⅔ cup flour
1 tablespoon salt
⅛ teaspoon pepper
3 pounds beef chuck, cut in 1½-inch cubes
⅓ cup salad oil
1 cup chopped onion
1 cup chopped celery
½ cup chopped green pepper
2 cloves garlic, crushed
2 cans (10½-ounce size) condensed beef consommé, undiluted

1 can (1 pound) tomatoes, undrained
1 can (6 ounces) tomato paste
2 tablespoons chopped parsley
2 teaspoons paprika
2 teaspoons Worcestershire sauce
12 new potatoes, scrubbed (about 1 pound)

1. On waxed paper, combine flour, salt, and pepper; use to coat beef cubes. Reserve remaining flour mixture.

2. In 3 tablespoons hot oil in Dutch oven, brown beef cubes, a third at a time. Remove as they are browned. Add more oil as needed.

3. Add onion, celery, green pepper, and garlic to drippings in Dutch oven; sauté until tender—about 5 minutes. Remove from heat.

4. Stir in reserved flour mixture, stirring until well blended. Gradually stir in consommé. Add tomatoes, tomato paste, parsley, paprika, Worcestershire, and browned beef.

5. Bring to boiling, stirring occasionally. Reduce heat, and simmer, covered 1¾ hours. Add potatoes, and cook, covered, 45 minutes longer, or until the potatoes and meat are tender. Sprinkle with more chopped parsley, if desired, before serving.

Makes 6 to 8 servings.

Ragout of Lamb

2 pounds shoulder of lean
   lamb, cut in 1-inch cubes
3 tablespoons flour
½ cup butter or margarine
1 teaspoon salt
¼ teaspoon pepper
1½ teaspoons dried oregano
1 can (13¾ ounces) chicken
   broth
1 can (6 ounces) tomato paste
1 teaspoon sugar

4 white turnips, quartered
8 small white onions, peeled
1 clove garlic, minced
4 small carrots, pared and cut
   in strips
1 leek, cut in large cubes
1 package (8 ounces) broad
   noodles
1 can (8½ ounces) peas, drained
¼ cup finely chopped parsley

1. Lightly coat lamb cubes with flour. In 3 tablespoons butter, in 4-quart Dutch oven or heavy kettle, brown lamb on all sides. Add salt, pepper, oregano, chicken broth, and tomato paste; cover, and let simmer for 45 minutes.

2. In small skillet, heat 3 tablespoons butter with sugar. Add turnips, onions, and garlic; cook over low heat until vegetables are glazed and light-golden.

3. Meanwhile, preheat oven to 350° F. Add glazed vegetables, carrots, and leek to browned meat; cover, and bake 1 hour. About 20 minutes before serving time, cook noodles according to package directions. Add peas and finely chopped parsley to lamb mixture.

4. To serve: Toss remaining 2 tablespoons butter or margarine with drained noodles. Arrange on heated serving platter, and top with Ragout of Lamb.

Makes 4 to 6 servings.

Lamb Ragout with Baked Eggplant

3 (1-pound size) eggplants
3 teaspoons salt
6 tablespoons butter or
   margarine

3 cups cubed cooked lamb (1¼
   pounds)
2 medium-size carrots, pared
   and diced

1 clove garlic, crushed
1 can (8 ounces) whole onions
1 can (6 ounces) tomato paste
1 chicken-bouillon cube
⅛ teaspoon pepper
¼ teaspoon dried thyme leaves

¼ teaspoon dried rosemary
  leaves
1 package (4⅛ ounces) instant
  mashed potato
1 cup milk
Paprika

1. Wash eggplants. Halve lengthwise. Make several deep gashes on cut side of each half, being careful not to cut through skin. Sprinkle with 1½ teaspoons salt. Let stand 30 minutes.

2. Preheat oven to 375° F. Drain eggplant halves; pat dry with paper towels. Place, cut sides down, in shallow roasting pan; add 1 cup boiling water.

3. Bake, uncovered, 15 minutes, or just until tender.

4. Cool eggplant on wire rack. Scoop out pulp, keeping shells intact. Chop pulp coarsely; drain; reserve.

5. In 2 tablespoons hot butter in large saucepan, sauté lamb, carrot, and garlic 5 minutes.

6. Drain onions, reserving liquid. Add water to liquid to measure 2 cups. Add to sautéed meat mixture with onions, tomato paste, bouillon cube, ½ teaspoon salt, the pepper, thyme, and rosemary.

7. Bring to boiling. Reduce heat, and simmer, covered, 30 minutes. Stir in reserved eggplant pulp.

8. Meanwhile, prepare mashed potato as package label directs, using only 1½ cups water and 1 cup milk, 1 teaspoon salt, and rest of butter.

9. Fill eggplant shells with meat mixture, mounding it. Place in shallow baking pan. Make a border of potato around edge of each eggplant half. (If desired, use pastry bag with decorating tip to make potato border.) Sprinkle potato with paprika.

10. Bake, uncovered, in 375° F. oven 15 minutes, or until heated through.

Makes 6 servings.

Turkey Ragout

Butter or margarine
1 large onion, sliced
2 medium-size zucchini, sliced
  (about 3 cups)
½ cup sliced celery
4 cups cooked turkey, in large
  chunks (about 1½-inch)
½ pound small fresh
  mushrooms, washed
1 can (1 pound) whole carrots,
  drained

⅔ cup dry white wine
⅔ cup canned condensed
  chicken broth, undiluted
1 can (10½ ounces) condensed
  cream of celery soup
1 can (10½ ounces) condensed
  cream of chicken soup
¼ teaspoon dried thyme
¼ teaspoon dried marjoram

Chopped parsley

1. Preheat oven to 350° F.
2. In 4 tablespoons hot butter in large, heavy skillet, sauté onion, zucchini, and celery until almost tender and lightly browned—about 10 to 15 minutes. Combine with turkey in a 3-quart casserole.
3. In same skillet, brown mushrooms, adding more butter if needed. Add to turkey mixture in casserole. Add carrots.
4. Stir wine into drippings in skillet, then chicken broth, celery soup, chicken soup, thyme, and marjoram. Bring to boiling, stirring to loosen browned bits in pan. Pour wine mixture over turkey and vegetables in casserole, and mix lightly with a fork.
5. Bake, covered, 1 hour, or until bubbling in center. Sprinkle with chopped parsley.
Makes 6 servings.

Beef Goulash

¼ cup salad oil
3 pounds beef chuck
4 medium-size onions, finely
  chopped
¼ cup tomato paste
¼ cup chopped parsley
2 teaspoons salt

1 teaspoon dried thyme leaves
¼ teaspoon pepper
1 small bay leaf

Hot buttered noodles (optional)

1. Heat oil in 6-quart Dutch oven. Cut pieces of beef in 1½-inch cubes. Add to Dutch oven, a third at a time, and brown on all sides; remove as browned.

2. Preheat oven to 300° F.

3. Add onion to pan drippings, and sauté until golden brown—about 10 minutes. Return the browned meat to pan.

4. Stir in 1½ cups water, the tomato paste, parsley, salt, thyme, pepper, and bay leaf; bring to boiling.

5. Bake, covered, 2 hours, or until beef is tender. Nice with buttered noodles.

Makes 8 servings.

Party Beef Goulash

½ cup salad oil	2 tablespoons paprika
6 pounds chuck, trimmed and cut into 1-inch cubes	3 tablespoons brown sugar
	1 tablespoon salt
1 cup chopped onion	2 teaspoons Worcestershire sauce
2 cloves garlic, peeled and crushed	
	2 teaspoons wine vinegar
1 cup catsup	¼ cup unsifted all-purpose flour
⅓ cup chili sauce	
¾ teaspoon dry mustard	Hot noodles (optional)

1. Heat some of oil in large Dutch oven. Add beef cubes (about a fourth at a time), onion, and garlic. Brown beef well on all sides, adding more oil as needed. Remove beef as it browns; continue until all beef is browned.

2. Add 3 cups water and remaining ingredients, except flour; stir until well combined. Put beef back into Dutch oven; simmer, covered, about 2 hours, or until tender.

3. Combine flour and ¼ cup water in small bowl, stirring until smooth. Stir into hot beef mixture; cook, stirring, until goulash returns to boiling and is thick.

4. Serve over noodles, if desired.

Makes 12 servings.

Note: This may be prepared the day before and refrigerated. Before serving the goulash, reheat slowly.

Veal Goulash

2 tablespoons butter or margarine	1 tablespoon brown sugar
2 pounds stewing veal, in ¾-inch cubes	6 new potatoes, peeled
1 can (1 pound) whole carrots	1 can (8 ounces) small white onions, drained
1 can (8 ounces) tomato sauce with mushrooms	1½ cups dairy sour cream
1 envelope (1⅝₁₆ ounces) Sloppy-Joe-seasoning mix	Chopped parsley

1. In hot butter in 4-quart Dutch oven, quickly brown veal, half at a time; remove as browned. When all is browned, return to Dutch oven.

2. Drain liquid from carrots, and stir liquid into veal, along with tomato sauce, seasoning mix, and brown sugar. Bring to boiling.

3. Add potatoes; reduce heat, and simmer, covered and stirring occasionally, until meat and potatoes are tender—about 30 minutes. Add drained carrots and onions; simmer 5 minutes longer.

4. Stir in sour cream until well blended. Heat, but do not boil. Turn into serving dish; sprinkle with parsley.

Makes 6 servings.

V

Some Have a Foreign Accent

❀ ❀ ❀

Too often homemakers serve the same familiar standbys over and over. It's easy to prepare identical menus week after week—the butcher knows just what to put aside for his customer; his customer knows how long she's going to have to spend in the kitchen, and the family members have a pretty good idea of what not to have for lunch unless they want to eat the same thing twice in one day.

Yet the chops-on-Monday, tuna-on-Tuesday, hamburger-on-Wednesday routine not only does away with the joy of anticipating a delicious meal, it acts as a damper on appetites and dispositions. It's difficult to be hungry *and* witty when you're staring at frankfurters and beans for the fourth time in as many weeks.

The solution, of course, is variety in meal planning, and when that variety involves recipes from foreign countries, so much the better. Foods of other lands can be fun to prepare and appetizing to eat, and they may even spark new table conversation. What husband confronted with a Vitello Tonnato with Sicilian Tomatoes plus Zabaglione for dessert would dare ask the question "What's new?"

It is not necessary, however, to plunge the household suddenly into a dizzying succession of unfamiliar tastes such as tortillas, bouillabaisse, and sukiyaki. Moderation in introducing new foods is just as important as inventiveness in menus.

It goes without saying that international dishes can be doubly meaningful when there are young students in the family. If the geography lesson happens to involve China, an authentic Chinese dinner complete with chopsticks and a discussion of the various regional cuisines will have a definite impact on both appetites and homework. Or if History II is reviewing French kings, everyone, including Mother, will get better marks after a classic Boeuf Bourguignon and that favorite of Louis XIV, Pot de Crème au Chocolat. Devoting one night a month to a foreign cuisine, and to a discussion of the country, its foods, and its customs, can be an enjoyable family activity, as well as a happy dining experience.

If you've ever tried to learn a foreign language, you're aware of the fact that you first have to study the basic rules of grammar and pronunciation. When you attempt to prepare foreign dishes, it's important to acquaint yourself with the special ingredients or the different techniques of preparation that are required. A good start is a visit to your local library or bookshop, where you'll find cookbooks devoted to foreign cuisines such as French, Italian, German, Greek, Spanish, and Chinese.

Next, check the ethnic food shops in your area. Take time to explore their aromatic interiors, and become familiar with the distinctive wares on their shelves. A wide variety of foreign foods, such as canned meats and vegetables, rare spices, native condiments, and tropical fruits, are available in stores throughout the United States, and the American homemaker can reproduce many foreign specialties as they would be prepared in their country of origin.

When you set out to master recipes from other countries, don't immediately try to make the most elaborate dishes, the ones that are special to fine restaurants. Concentrate, instead, on the simple fare, the popular home favorites. And don't be frightened by the names of certain recipes. You'll discover that the recipe makers of other lands have often been very imaginative. Some vivid examples: England's "Bubble and Squeak" (leftover beef and cabbage); "Spotted Dog" (Irish soda bread with raisins in it); Italy's "Little Rags Soup," or

Stracciatella, which is a broth with delicate shreds of egg not unlike Chinese egg drop soup; or "Lost Bread," the French name for stale bread that is soaked in milk and eggs, then fried.

You'll learn, too, that many foreign dishes have traditional accompaniments or garnishes. With a carbonnade of beef, for example, one must always serve beer; with Viennese boiled beef, an apple and horseradish sauce is de rigueur. The German oxtail soup is seldom served without macaroons, and sauerbraten traditionally is accompanied by potato pancakes and red cabbage.

As you continue to add foreign dishes to your working repertoire, you'll find that you are on the way to becoming a citizen of the world. One friend of ours made a study of Polynesian cooking and became so knowledgeable about it that her husband surprised her with an anniversary trip to Hawaii. Unfortunately, she would have preferred to see Rome. "Why didn't I specialize in pasta instead of poi?" she mourned.

So be advised: if you are yearning for a holiday in Sweden, don't become the best borsch maker on your block.

Beef Balls Bourguignon

2½ pounds ground chuck
1 teaspoon salt
¼ teaspoon pepper
1 tablespoon butter or
    margarine
3 tablespoons brandy
½ pound small fresh
    mushrooms, washed
½ pound small white onions,
    peeled

2 tablespoons flour
½ cup canned condensed beef
    bouillon, undiluted
1 cup Burgundy
½ cup ruby port
1 teaspoon meat-extract paste
2 tablespoons tomato paste
1 bay leaf

Hot noodles (optional)

1. Lightly mix beef with salt and pepper. Shape into 24 meatballs, about 2 inches in diameter. In hot butter in 6-quart Dutch oven, brown meatballs well all over.

2. Heat brandy in small saucepan until bubbles form around edge of pan. Ignite with match, and pour over meatballs. When flame dies out, remove meatballs from Dutch oven with slotted spoon.

3. Add mushrooms to drippings in Dutch oven; sauté until lightly browned—about 5 minutes. Remove mushrooms, and add to meatballs.

4. Add onions to Dutch oven; sauté until lightly browned—about 5 minutes. Remove from heat. Stir in flour, then bouillon, wines, meat-extract paste, tomato paste, and bay leaf.

5. Cook, stirring frequently, until thickened. Reduce heat; simmer, covered, 10 minutes. Add meatballs and mushrooms to mixture; simmer, covered and stirring occasionally, 30 minutes longer.

6. If desired, serve with noodles.

Makes 8 servings.

Beef Balls Bourguignon en Croûte

2 or 3 slices white bread, broken into small pieces (1 cup)

¾ cup canned condensed beef broth, undiluted

2½ pounds ground chuck

1 teaspoon salt

¼ teaspoon pepper

1 egg, slightly beaten

3 tablespoons butter or margarine

3 tablespoons brandy

½ pound small fresh mushrooms, washed and halved

½ pound small white onions, peeled and quartered

2 tablespoons flour

1 cup Burgundy

½ cup ruby port

1 teaspoon meat-extract paste or granulated beef bouillon

2 tablespoons tomato paste

1 bay leaf

1 long loaf Italian bread (18 inches long and 5 inches wide)

¼ cup butter or margarine, melted

Chopped parsley (optional)

Watercress sprigs (optional)

1. In a large bowl, soak bread pieces in ¼ cup beef broth 10 minutes. Add beef, salt, pepper, and egg; toss lightly with fork until well combined.

2. Shape beef mixture, handling lightly, into 50 small meatballs 1 inch in diameter.

3. In 3 tablespoons hot butter in large Dutch oven, brown meatballs, about a third at a time, until browned well all over, removing them as they brown. When all are browned, return to Dutch oven.

4. Heat brandy in small saucepan until bubbles form around edge of pan. Ignite with match, and pour over meatballs. When flame dies out, remove meatballs from Dutch oven with slotted spoon.

5. Add mushrooms to drippings in Dutch oven; sauté until lightly browned—about 5 minutes. Remove mushrooms, and add to meatballs.

6. Add onions to Dutch oven; sauté until lightly browned—about 5 minutes. Remove from heat. Stir in flour, then remaining beef broth, wines, meat-extract paste, tomato paste, and bay leaf.

7. Cook, stirring frequently, until thickened. Reduce heat; simmer, covered, 10 minutes. Add meatballs and mushrooms to mixture; simmer, covered and stirring occasionally, 30 minutes longer.

8. Meanwhile, prepare bread: Preheat oven to 350° F. Using a serrated bread knife, slice off top of bread lengthwise. Hollow out loaf, leaving a shell 1 inch thick. Brush inside with melted butter; wrap in foil; bake 15 minutes.

9. To serve: Make crosswise cuts in bread at 3-inch intervals but not through to bottom. Arrange on board; fill loaf with beef balls, mounding high; pour some of sauce over top. If desired, sprinkle with chopped parsley, and garnish with watercress. Serve with toothpicks; or cut through bread completely, and serve beef balls with the bread. Pass rest of sauce.

Makes 6 to 8 servings.

Note: The beef balls may be made ahead through Step 7 and frozen, or stored in refrigerator a few days, then reheated slowly for serving.

Coq au Vin

1 (5-pound size) roasting chicken	1 clove garlic, crushed
4 slices bacon, cut in 1-inch pieces	2 tablespoons brandy
	2⅓ cups red Burgundy
4 tablespoons butter or margarine	1 can (10½ ounces) condensed chicken broth, undiluted
¼ cup chopped shallot	1 teaspoon salt
	¼ teaspoon dried thyme leaves

⅛ teaspoon pepper
1 bay leaf
2 large sprigs parsley
Tops from 2 celery stalks
12 small new potatoes
12 small white onions, peeled

12 medium-size fresh
mushrooms, washed
4 tablespoons flour

2 tablespoons chopped parsley

1. Wash chicken; pat dry with paper towels.

2. In 6-quart Dutch oven, sauté bacon until crisp. Remove bacon; reserve. Pour fat into a cup. Return 2 tablespoons fat to Dutch oven; add 2 tablespoons butter.

3. In hot butter mixture, brown chicken well on all sides. Remove.

4. Add shallot and garlic; sauté until golden. Return chicken, breast side up, to Dutch oven. In large cooking spoon, warm brandy; ignite, and pour over chicken.

5. When flame dies, turn chicken breast side down. Add 2 cups wine, the chicken broth, salt, thyme, pepper, bay leaf, parsley sprigs, and celery; bring to boiling. Reduce heat, and simmer, covered, 30 minutes.

6. Meanwhile, scrub potatoes; pare a narrow band of skin around center of each.

7. In medium-size skillet, in 2 tablespoons hot butter, brown onions. Remove as browned; set aside. Add mushrooms to skillet, and sauté.

8. Turn chicken breast side up. Add potatoes, onions, and mushrooms to Dutch oven; simmer, covered, 45 to 50 minutes, or until chicken and vegetables are tender.

9. Remove chicken, potatoes, onions, and mushrooms to heated serving platter. Sprinkle bacon over vegetables. Keep warm.

10. Remove and discard celery, parsley, and bay leaf. Measure liquid in Dutch oven; it should measure 3 cups. (If more than 3 cups, reduce by boiling.)

11. Blend flour with remaining ⅓ cup Burgundy. Stir into pan liquid; bring to boiling, stirring; boil until sauce thickens; simmer 5 minutes.

12. Spoon some sauce over chicken and vegetables; pour rest into sauceboat. Sprinkle chopped parsley over vegetables.

Makes 6 servings.

Chicken and Rice, Basque Style

1   pound hot Italian sausages
1   cup chicken stock, fresh or
    canned
A strip of orange peel (removed
    with a rotary peeler), 1 inch
    wide by 3 inches long
4   tablespoons olive oil
2   medium-size green peppers,
    seeded and cut into julienne
    strips, ½ inch by 1½ inches
1   teaspoon finely chopped
    garlic
1½ pounds firm ripe tomatoes,
    peeled, seeded, and coarsely
    chopped

2   teaspoons paprika
1   teaspoon dried oregano
Salt
Freshly ground black pepper
5   cups cooked rice (1⅔ cups
    raw rice), cold
1   teaspoon butter
4 to 6 substantial pieces of cold
    roast chicken: wings, thighs,
    breasts, etc. (substantial
    scraps will do if they must)

1   tablespoon parsley, finely
    chopped

1. Choose a heavy frying pan just about large enough to hold the sausages, and cover them with the cup of chicken stock—or a little more, if necessary. Add orange peel, and bring stock to a boil.

2. Turn the heat down to moderate; let sausages simmer for about 5 minutes; then prick them with the point of a knife, to allow the fat to escape.

3. Pierce them again after 5 more minutes of cooking. Then remove the sausages from the pan, and let them drain and cool on paper toweling. Reserve the chicken stock, but first skim off any fat.

4. Heat olive oil in a small, heavy frying pan, and cook the julienned green peppers over moderate heat for about 10 minutes, or until tender.

5. Add chopped garlic; cook for 1 or 2 minutes without browning. Then add thoroughly drained chopped tomatoes.

6. Mix in paprika, oregano, and salt and freshly ground pepper to taste, and cook vegetables quickly for about 5 minutes. Stir them almost constantly, and take care not to burn them.

7. When most of the liquid has cooked away, remove pan from heat.

8. Preheat oven to 350° F.

9. Arrange cooked rice (first seasoned with salt) in a lightly buttered 3- or 4-quart flameproof casserole. Pour over it ½ cup of reserved chicken-sausage stock.

10. Place chicken pieces on top, and spread tomato-pepper sauce around and between them. Slice sausages into ½-inch pieces, and arrange them around edge of casserole.

11. Bring to a boil on top of stove; then transfer casserole to center of oven, and let it bake, uncovered, for about 20 minutes, or until chicken is heated through.

12. Sprinkle with parsley, and serve directly from casserole.
Makes 4 to 6 servings.

Chicken Mexicana

1   (2½- to 3-pound size) broiler-fryer, cut up
½   cup butter or margarine
1   teaspoon salt
½   teaspoon paprika
Dash pepper
1   package (6 ounces) tortilla chips

1   can (4½ ounces) enchilada sauce
1   cup shredded Cheddar cheese
½   cup chopped green onion
1   can (2¼ ounces) pitted black olives, sliced

1. Preheat oven to 375° F.

2. Wash chicken under cold water; dry with paper towels. Arrange in single layer, skin side up, in a large, shallow baking pan (14 by 10 inches).

3. Melt butter; pour over chicken; then sprinkle with salt, paprika, and pepper. Bake, uncovered, 60 minutes.

4. Crumble tortilla chips coarsely; sprinkle over chicken. Add enchilada sauce; sprinkle evenly with cheese, then onion and olives. Return to oven 15 minutes, or until cheese is melted.
Makes 6 servings.

Arroz con Pollo

1 (3-pound size) broiler-fryer, cut in 8 pieces
½ cup olive oil
2 cups chopped onion
1 clove garlic, crushed
½ teaspoon crushed red pepper
2½ teaspoons salt
½ teaspoon pepper
2 cups raw converted white rice
¼ teaspoon saffron threads
1 can (1 pound, 12 ounces) tomatoes, undrained

1 canned green chili pepper, chopped
1 can (10½ ounces) condensed chicken broth, undiluted
½ package (10-ounce size) frozen peas
½ cup pimiento-stuffed green olives, sliced
1 can (4 ounces) pimientos, drained and sliced

1. Wipe chicken pieces with damp paper towels.

2. In heavy 6-quart Dutch oven, heat olive oil. Brown chicken, a few pieces at a time, until golden brown all over. Remove chicken as it browns.

3. Preheat oven to 325° F.

4. Add chopped onion, garlic, and red pepper to Dutch oven; sauté, stirring, over medium heat until onion is golden—about 3 minutes.

5. Add salt, pepper, rice, and saffron to Dutch oven; cook, stirring, until rice is lightly browned—about 10 minutes.

6. Add tomatoes, chili pepper, and chicken broth to rice mixture. Add chicken pieces. Bring just to boiling.

7. Bake, covered, 1 hour.

8. Add ½ cup water. Sprinkle peas, olives, and pimiento strips over top; do not stir. Bake, covered, 20 minutes longer, or until chicken is tender and peas are cooked.

9. Serve hot right from Dutch oven.

Makes 6 servings.

Paella Valenciana

2 tablespoons salad oil
4 small whole chicken breasts, split (about 2 pounds in all)

3 cloves garlic, crushed
2 cups coarsely chopped green pepper

2 cups chopped onion
¼ cup chopped parsley
½ teaspoon crumbled saffron
1 tablespoon paprika
1 teaspoon dried oregano leaves
Salt
¼ teaspoon pepper
4 chicken-bouillon cubes

2 cups bottled clam juice
2 cups raw long-grain white rice
4 (8-ounce size) frozen
   rock-lobster tails
16 littleneck clams, in the shell,
   scrubbed

Lemon wedges (optional)

1. Slowly heat oil in heavy 6-quart Dutch oven. In hot oil, lightly brown chicken on all sides. Remove chicken from Dutch oven.

2. In drippings, sauté garlic, green pepper, onion, and parsley 10 minutes, stirring.

3. Add saffron, paprika, oregano, ¾ teaspoon salt, and the pepper; mix well. Add bouillon cubes, clam juice, and 4 cups water; bring to boiling, stirring.

4. Stir in rice; then add chicken pieces; return to boiling. Reduce heat; simmer, covered and stirring occasionally, 30 minutes, or until the chicken pieces and the rice are tender.

5. Meanwhile, in large kettle, bring 2 quarts water to boiling. Add 1 tablespoon salt and the lobster tails; return to boiling.

6. Cover kettle; simmer lobster tails 5 minutes.

7. Add unshelled clams to kettle; simmer 5 minutes longer, or until the clam shells open and the lobster is tender.

8. With tongs, remove clams and lobster from kettle. With kitchen shears, cut undershells from lobster tails.

9. To serve: Turn rice and chicken onto large serving platter. Arrange lobster tails over rice.

10. Drain clams; arrange, still in shells, over rice. Serve with lemon wedges, if desired.

Makes 8 servings.

Maharani Chicken Curry

1 (2- to 2½-pound size) broiler-fryer, cut up	1 (2-inch) stick cinnamon
¼ cup butter or margarine	Seeds from 1 small cardamom pod
1½ cups chopped onion	Dash turmeric
½ clove garlic, chopped	Dash ground cumin
1½ teaspoons ground ginger	Dash paprika
1 cup diced fresh tomato (1 large)	Dash pepper
1 teaspoon salt	⅓ cup plain yogurt

1. Wash chicken; dry with paper towels. Remove skin, and discard.

2. In hot butter in large skillet with tight-fitting cover, sauté chicken until nicely browned all over—10 to 15 minutes; remove. Add onion, and sauté with garlic and ginger until golden—about 10 minutes.

3. Add tomato, salt, cinnamon, cardamom, turmeric, cumin, paprika, and pepper; cook over low heat 3 minutes. Add yogurt; stir until well blended. Add chicken pieces.

4. Simmer, covered and turning chicken occasionally, 30 to 40 minutes, or until fork-tender. Arrange chicken on platter; spoon on sauce.

Makes 4 servings.

Hungarian Goulash with Galuska

2 tablespoons butter or margarine	⅛ teaspoon pepper
2 tablespoons salad oil	1 bay leaf
2 pounds boneless veal, cut in 1-inch cubes	1 can (10½ ounces) condensed beef bouillon, undiluted
1 cup sliced onion	2 tablespoons tomato paste
1 cup green-pepper strips	2 tablespoons flour
⅓ cup thinly sliced celery	½ cup dairy sour cream
1 clove garlic, crushed	
1 cup thinly sliced carrots	Chopped parsley (optional)
2 to 3 teaspoons paprika	
1½ teaspoons salt	Galuska (see p. 143)

1. Heat 1 tablespoon butter and 1 tablespoon salad oil in 4-quart Dutch oven over medium heat. Add a few pieces of veal, and brown well on all sides. Remove to a bowl. Repeat with rest of veal, adding remaining butter and salad oil as needed.

2. In drippings, sauté onion, green pepper, celery, and garlic until tender—about 3 minutes.

3. Stir in carrots, paprika, salt, pepper, bay leaf, bouillon, tomato paste, and browned veal. Bring to boiling; reduce heat; simmer, covered, 50 minutes, or until veal is fork-tender. Remove Dutch oven from heat.

4. With slotted spoon, remove veal and vegetables to hot serving platter; keep warm. Pour pan liquid into 1-cup measure; if necessary, add water to make 1 cup.

5. Add flour to Dutch oven; gradually add reserved liquid, stirring constantly. Cook over moderate heat, stirring, until mixture boils. Reduce heat; simmer 3 minutes.

6. Stir in sour cream. Heat slightly. Pour over veal and vegetables. Garnish with chopped parsley, if desired. Serve with Galuska.

Makes 4 to 6 servings.

Galuska

3 **cups sifted all-purpose flour**	1 **tablespoon butter or**
2 **eggs**	**margarine, melted**
3 **teaspoons salt**	

1. In large bowl, combine flour with eggs, 1 teaspoon salt, and 1 cup water; with wooden spoon, stir until smooth. Gradually add ¼ cup water, beating until dough is almost runny and bubbles appear on surface.

2. In 4-quart kettle, bring 2 quarts water and 2 teaspoons salt to boiling.

3. Put half of dough into a coarse colander. Holding colander over boiling salted water and using wooden spoon, stir dough through holes. Boil, uncovered, until dumplings rise to top and are just firm. With slotted spoon, lift out dumplings to warm serving dish. Keep warm until serving.

4. Repeat with rest of dough. Toss the cooked dumplings with the melted butter. Serve with Hungarian Goulash.

Makes 4 to 6 servings.

Meatballs Parmigiana

1 package (8 ounces) wide
noodles
2 tablespoons salad oil
1 small onion, sliced
1 can (1 pound) tomatoes,
undrained
1 can (15½ ounces) spaghetti
sauce with mushrooms
1 egg

⅓ cup soft white-bread crumbs
1 pound ground chuck
½ cup grated Parmesan cheese
¼ teaspoon dried oregano leaves
1 teaspoon salt
Dash pepper
½ package (8-ounce size) sliced
mozzarella cheese

1. Cook noodles as package label directs; drain. Arrange in 12- by 8-
by 2-inch baking dish.
2. Meanwhile, in hot oil in large skillet, sauté onion until
tender—about 3 minutes. Add tomatoes and spaghetti sauce; bring to
boiling over medium heat.
3. In medium-size bowl, combine egg, ¼ cup water, the bread
crumbs, chuck, ¼ cup Parmesan, the oregano, salt, and pepper; mix
lightly. Shape into 24 meatballs.
4. Add meatballs to boiling sauce; simmer, covered, 20 minutes.
Preheat oven to 350° F.
5. Spoon meatballs over noodles in baking dish. Cover with cheese
slices; pour on sauce. Sprinkle remaining Parmesan over top.
6. Bake, uncovered, 20 minutes, or until golden brown and heated
through.
Makes 6 servings.

Polish Meatball Casserole with Sour-Cream Sauce

Potato Border

1 package (7 ounces) instant
mashed potato
¼ cup butter or margarine

2 teaspoons salt
1 cup milk

Meatballs

1½ pounds lean ground pork	1½ teaspoons salt
1 egg	½ teaspoon dried marjoram
½ cup packaged seasoned dry	leaves
bread crumbs	¼ teaspoon pepper
½ cup milk	2 tablespoons flour
½ cup finely chopped onion	2 tablespoons salad oil

Sour-Cream Sauce

2 tablespoons flour	¼ cup grated Parmesan cheese
1 beef-bouillon cube	
½ cup dairy sour cream	Parsley
2 teaspoons lemon juice	

1. Make Potato Border: Prepare both envelopes mashed potato as package label directs, using amount of water specified on package and the amounts of butter, salt, and milk listed on page 144. Set aside.

2. Make Meatballs: In large bowl, combine pork, egg, bread crumbs, milk, onion, salt, marjoram, and pepper; mix lightly until well blended. Shape into balls about 1½ inches in diameter.

3. Preheat oven to 350° F. Roll meatballs in flour, coating completely.

4. In hot oil in skillet, sauté meatballs until browned on all sides. Remove, as they brown, to a 2-quart casserole or shallow baking dish; mound in center.

5. Make Sour-Cream Sauce: Measure drippings in skillet; add more oil, if necessary, to make 2 tablespoons. Return to skillet; stir in flour until smooth. Gradually stir in 1 cup water and the bouillon cube.

6. Bring to boiling. Remove from heat. Add sour cream and lemon juice, stirring to combine; return to heat and simmer 2 minutes. Remove from heat.

7. Spoon mashed potato around meatballs in casserole; sprinkle potato with cheese. Pour sauce over meatballs.

8. Bake, uncovered, 1 hour, or until potato is golden brown. Garnish with parsley.

Makes 8 servings.

Sweet and Pungent Meatballs

Meatballs

1 slice white bread
1½ pounds ground chuck
1 teaspoon salt
¼ teaspoon ginger
1 teaspoon soy sauce*

¼ teaspoon Tabasco
1 can (5 ounces) water
    chestnuts, drained and diced

2 tablespoons salad or olive oil

Sauce

¼ cup cider vinegar
¾ cup canned condensed beef
    bouillon, undiluted
1 tablespoon catsup
1 tablespoon soy sauce*
1 tablespoon molasses
¼ cup light-brown sugar, firmly
    packed
1 package (13¼ ounces) frozen
    pineapple chunks, thawed
    and drained

½ cup preserved kumquats,
    drained
2 tablespoons cornstarch
½ cup green-pepper strips, 2
    inches long
⅓ cup watermelon-pickle
    rounds, drained
6 maraschino cherries

Cooked white rice
Soy sauce

1. Make Meatballs: Soak bread in water; then squeeze dry. In large bowl, combine bread, chuck, salt, ginger, 1 teaspoon soy sauce, the Tabasco, and water chestnuts. Toss lightly just to combine. Gently shape into 20 meatballs.

2. In hot oil in large skillet, sauté meatballs, turning, until nicely browned all over. Remove from heat, and set aside.

3. Make Sauce: In another large skillet or Dutch oven, combine vinegar, ½ cup water, the bouillon, catsup, 1 tablespoon soy sauce, the molasses, sugar, pineapple chunks, and kumquats; mix well. Bring to boiling.

4. Meanwhile, dissolve cornstarch in ¼ cup water; stir into boiling mixture. Boil, stirring, 2 minutes, or until mixture is thickened and translucent.

---

*Different brands of soy sauce vary slightly in strength. It may be necessary to use a little more or less, depending on the brand.

5. Add browned meatballs, pepper strips, watermelon pickle, and cherries; stir to combine. Cook just until heated through.

6. Serve over hot boiled rice, along with soy sauce.

Makes 5 or 6 servings.

Lamb, Armenian Style

6 carrots, pared
8 medium-size potatoes, pared and halved
1 small eggplant, cut in large chunks
2 onions, peeled and sliced
1 pound zucchini, cut in ½-inch slices
4 fresh tomatoes, halved; or 1 can (1 pound, 12 ounces) tomatoes

Few sprigs parsley, chopped
1 bay leaf
1 clove garlic, minced
2 teaspoons salt
½ teaspoon pepper
6 shoulder lamb chops, 1 inch thick
¼ cup all-purpose flour

1. Preheat oven to 375° F.

2. In deep baking dish (with cover) or Dutch oven, arrange carrots, potatoes, eggplant, onion, and zucchini. Top with tomatoes. (If using canned tomatoes, drain reserving ½ cup liquid.)

3. Combine parsley, bay leaf, half of garlic, 1½ teaspoons salt, and ¼ teaspoon pepper. Sprinkle over vegetables.

4. Wipe lamb chops with damp paper towels. Rub with remaining garlic, 1 teaspoon salt, and ¼ teaspoon pepper. Arrange on vegetables.

5. Bake, covered, 1 hour. Remove from oven.

6. Mix flour with ½ cup water (or reserved tomato liquid) until smooth. Lifting chops in several places, stir flour mixture into pan juices.

7. Bake, uncovered, 20 minutes longer, or until gravy is thickened and chops are brown.

8. To serve: Arrange lamb chops on platter, and surround with vegetables. Pass gravy separately.

Makes 6 servings.

Middle East Shish Kebabs

1 (5-pound size) leg of lamb,
cut into 1-inch cubes

Marinade

½ cup salad or olive oil
1 tablespoon salt
1 tablespoon black pepper
1½ teaspoons curry powder
3 cups sliced onion
½ teaspoon crushed red pepper
1 clove garlic, crushed
1 teaspoon dry mustard

1 cup dry red wine
2 tablespoons chopped parsley
1 cup chopped green pepper

1 pound sliced bacon (16 slices,
halved)
Arabic bread (optional)
Cooked white rice (optional)

1. If possible, have butcher cut lamb into cubes. Trim any fat and gristle from lamb. Place in large, deep bowl.

2. Make Marinade: Combine all marinade ingredients; mix well. Pour over lamb, tossing to coat well. Refrigerate, covered, overnight.

3. Next day, on each of 16 wooden hibachi sticks, thread 3 lamb cubes, alternately with 2 bacon pieces (see note). Arrange on broiler rack in broiler pan. Brush with any leftover marinade.

4. Broil, 4 inches from heat, 20 to 25 minutes, turning several times until lamb is cooked as you like it.

5. Serve shish kebabs hot, with Arabic bread or cooked white rice, if desired.

Makes 16 servings.

Note: Lamb and bacon cook better if they are not packed tightly together on skewers.

Pasta e Fagioli

1½ cups dried navy or pea beans
Salt
½ package (1-pound size) shell
macaroni (3 cups)

3 tablespoons olive oil
1 large onion, chopped
2 cups sliced carrot
1 cup chopped celery

1   clove garlic, crushed
2   cups diced peeled tomato (1
    pound)
1   teaspoon dried sage leaves
½   teaspoon dried oregano leaves
¼   teaspoon pepper

Chopped parsley
Grated Parmesan cheese

1. In a large bowl, combine beans with 6 cups cold water. Refrigerate overnight.

2. Next day, turn beans and water into 6-quart kettle. Add 1½ teaspoons salt.

3. Bring to boiling; reduce heat, and simmer, covered, about 3 hours, or until beans are tender. Stir several times during cooking. Drain, reserving liquid (there will be about 2½ cups).

4. Cook macaroni following package-label directions.

5. Meanwhile, in hot oil in large skillet, sauté onion, carrot, celery, and garlic, covered, until soft—about 20 minutes. Do not brown. Add tomato, sage, oregano, ½ teaspoon salt, and the pepper. Cover; cook, over medium heat, 15 minutes.

6. In large saucepan or kettle, combine beans, macaroni, and sautéed vegetables. Add 1½ cups reserved bean liquid. Bring to boiling; cover; simmer 35 to 40 minutes, stirring several times and adding more bean liquid if needed. Add salt and pepper if needed.

7. Turn into attractive serving dish or casserole. Sprinkle with chopped parsley and grated Parmesan cheese.

Makes 8 servings.

Italian-Sausage Polenta Pie

1½ pounds sweet Italian sausages
1   cup sliced onion
1   clove garlic, crushed
1   can (1 pound) tomatoes,
    undrained
1   can (8 ounces) tomato sauce
¾   teaspoon salt
½   teaspoon dried oregano leaves

½   teaspoon sugar
¼   teaspoon dried basil leaves
⅛   teaspoon pepper

1½ cups yellow cornmeal
¾   teaspoon salt
1   cup grated sharp Cheddar
    cheese

1. Brown sausages in large skillet. Reduce heat; cook sausages, turning occasionally, 15 minutes longer. Remove to paper towels to drain.

2. Pour off all but 1 tablespoon fat from skillet, and discard. In remaining fat in skillet, sauté onion and garlic until golden—about 5 minutes.

3. Halve 6 sausages lengthwise; set aside for top. Slice the rest.

4. Add tomatoes, tomato sauce, ¾ teaspoon salt, the oregano, sugar, basil, pepper, and sausage slices to onion mixture. Bring to boiling; reduce heat; simmer, uncovered and stirring occasionally, 25 minutes.

5. Preheat oven to 375° F.

6. In medium-size saucepan, combine cornmeal with 3 cups water and ¾ teaspoon salt. Bring to boiling, stirring constantly; boil until thickened—2 minutes. Remove from heat; let cool about 5 minutes.

7. Layer half the cornmeal mixture in a 2½-quart casserole; top with half the sausage mixture; sprinkle with half the cheese. Repeat. Arrange reserved sausage halves on top.

8. Bake, uncovered, 30 minutes, or until heated through.

Makes 6 servings.

Jamaican Rice and Beans

1 cup dry red kidney beans	1 cup chopped onion
1 quart boiling water	1 cup chopped red or green
3½ teaspoons salt	pepper
2 pounds coconut or 1 package	1 cup chopped celery
(7 ounces) flaked coconut	1 teaspoon dried thyme leaves
1 quart boiling water	⅛ teaspoon crushed red pepper
10 slices bacon, coarsely	¼ teaspoon black pepper
chopped	2 cups raw converted white rice
	2 cups diced peeled tomato

1. Wash beans; turn into a 2-quart saucepan. Add 1 quart boiling water and 1 teaspoon salt. Bring to boiling; boil, uncovered, 2 minutes. Remove from heat; let stand, uncovered, at room temperature 1 hour. Meanwhile, make coconut milk (see note).

2. Return beans to heat; bring to boiling; reduce heat, and simmer, covered, 1½ hours, or until beans are tender. Set aside.

3. Meanwhile, in 5-quart Dutch oven, over medium heat, sauté bacon until crisp. Drain bacon on paper towels. Pour off fat, reserving ¼ cup.

4. In ¼ cup hot bacon fat in Dutch oven, sauté onion, chopped pepper, celery, thyme leaves, and red and black pepper 5 minutes. Add bacon, 3½ cups coconut milk, and 2½ teaspoons salt. Over high heat, bring to boiling; stir in rice. Return to boiling; reduce heat; simmer, covered, 20 to 25 minutes, or until rice is cooked and liquid is absorbed.

5. Add drained kidney beans and the tomato to rice mixture, tossing gently with fork to mix well. Garnish with shredded coconut, if desired. Serve at once. Nice with chicken or beef dishes.

Makes 10 to 12 servings.

Note: To prepare coconut milk: Crack open coconut, reserving milk. Remove coconut meat; grate on coarse grater or grate small pieces in electric blender. Or use packaged flaked coconut. Line large strainer with cheesecloth, and place over a large bowl. Pour 1 quart boiling water over grated fresh coconut or flaked coconut in cheesecloth; let stand 1 hour. Squeeze pulp gently in cheesecloth to press out the liquid. Discard pulp. Add reserved coconut milk to that in bowl; measure; if necessary, add water to make 3½ cups.

Chili Tacos

2 pounds ground chuck	1 can (6 ounces) tomato paste
3 tablespoons butter or margarine	1 can (10½ ounces) condensed beef broth, undiluted
3 cups chopped onion	2 beef-bouillon cubes
2 cups chopped green pepper	4 packages (9-ounce size) frozen tortillas
3 cloves garlic, finely chopped	Salad oil for frying
2½ tablespoons chili powder	2 cans (4-ounce size) pimientos, drained and chopped
2 teaspoons cumin seed	3 quarts shredded lettuce
½ teaspoon salt	3 cups coarsely grated Cheddar cheese
¼ teaspoon black pepper	
1 teaspoon paprika	
1 bay leaf, crumbled	
2 cans (1-pound size) tomatoes, undrained	

1. In 5-quart Dutch oven, sauté beef until it loses pink color, stirring to break into small pieces as it browns. With slotted spoon, remove browned beef to bowl. Drain fat from Dutch oven, and discard.

2. In hot butter in same Dutch oven, sauté onion, green pepper, and garlic, over medium heat and stirring occasionally, about 5 minutes, or until onion is golden.

3. Stir in chili powder, cumin, salt, pepper, paprika, and bay leaf; simmer, stirring, several minutes.

4. Add browned beef, tomatoes, tomato paste, beef broth, and bouillon cubes. Stir, breaking up tomatoes. Bring to boiling; reduce heat, and simmer, uncovered and stirring occasionally, ½ hour.

5. Meanwhile, thaw frozen tortillas as package label directs. Then, in ½ inch hot oil in skillet, heat tortillas, as package label directs to make tacos.

6. To serve: Heat chili mixture to boiling. Stir in pimiento. Place about ¼ cup shredded lettuce in bottom of each taco. Spoon ¼ cup chili over lettuce; sprinkle with 1 tablespoon grated cheese. Serve at once.

Makes 48; 12 to 16 servings.

Note: The chili may be made ahead through Step 4 and frozen, or stored a few days in refrigerator, and reheated for serving.

Shrimp Asopao

¼ **cup olive oil**	2 **cups raw converted white rice**
1½ **cups finely chopped onion**	3 **pounds large raw shrimp,**
1½ **cups finely chopped green**	**shelled and deveined**
pepper	1 **package (10 ounces) frozen**
¼ **pound bacon, chopped**	**peas**
1 **(¼-pound) piece salt pork,**	½ **cup capers, drained**
cut to rind	½ **cup sliced stuffed green olives**
6 **cans (10½-ounce size)**	2 **pimientos, sliced**
condensed chicken broth,	
undiluted	

1. Slowly heat olive oil in 6- to 8-quart kettle. Add onion, green pepper, bacon, and salt pork. Cook, covered, over low heat 10 minutes.

2. Add chicken broth, 6 soup cans water. Bring to boil; add rice; return to boil; reduce heat; cook, covered, stirring occasionally, 30 minutes.

3. Add shrimp; bring to boiling; reduce heat, and simmer 15 minutes. Add frozen peas, capers, olives, and pimientos. Return to boiling; reduce heat, and cook 5 minutes, or until peas are tender. Discard salt pork.

4. Serve in deep soup plates.

Makes about 5 quarts; 10 to 12 main-dish servings.

Oriental Shrimp Casserole

1 tablespoon butter or
   margarine
1 cup thinly sliced celery
1 cup thinly sliced green pepper
1 can (8¾ ounces) pineapple
   tidbits
1 package (1¾ ounces) dry
   cream of leek soup mix
1 tablespoon cider vinegar

1 tablespoon light-brown sugar
2 teaspoons soy sauce
3 packages (7-ounce size)
   frozen shelled, deveined
   shrimp
1 cup Chinese noodles

Hot cooked fluffy white rice
Soy sauce

1. Preheat oven to 375° F.

2. In hot butter in medium-size skillet, sauté celery and green pepper until slightly tender but still crisp—about 5 minutes. Set aside.

3. Drain pineapple, reserving liquid. Add water to reserved liquid to measure 2 cups.

4. In medium-size saucepan, combine soup mix with reserved pineapple liquid, vinegar, brown sugar, and 2 teaspoons soy sauce; bring to boiling, stirring. Reduce heat; simmer 3 minutes.

5. Cook shrimp as package label directs; drain.

6. In 1½-quart casserole, combine sautéed vegetables, pineapple, soup mixture, and shrimp. Sprinkle top of casserole with Chinese noodles.

7. Bake, uncovered, about 20 minutes, or until sauce is bubbly. Serve over hot rice, with additional soy sauce.

Makes 4 to 6 servings.

Teriyaki

1¼ cups cream sherry
1 cup soy sauce
¼ cup canned condensed
   chicken broth, undiluted

1¼ pounds flank steak
1 can (15¼ ounces) pineapple
   chunks, drained
20 preserved kumquats, drained

1. In small saucepan, combine sherry, soy sauce, and chicken broth. Bring just to boiling; remove from heat. Pour into a shallow, 2-quart baking dish; let cool.

2. Meanwhile, wipe flank steak with damp paper towels. Trim off excess fat. Slice steak across the grain on the diagonal to make about 24 slices ¼ inch thick.

3. Arrange steak slices in marinade; refrigerate, covered, 2 hours or longer.

4. Just before cooking, cut steak slices into 1½-inch squares. Thread on 20 hibachi sticks, alternating steak squares with pineapple and kumquats.

5. Broil, on hibachi or in broiler, about 2 minutes per side. Serve at once.

Makes about 20; 5 servings.

VI

Top It with a Crust, Dot It with Dumplings

❀ ❀ ❀

Gift wrapping has become a year-round art, not just a holiday event. If you don't believe it, take a look at the variety of vividly designed wrapping papers and the rainbow of ribbons available at greeting-card and gift shops everywhere. There's a good reason—everyone loves to receive a gift that's imaginatively wrapped. It's all part of setting a mood, increasing the pleasure of the gift-getter and the pride of the gift-giver. Indeed, sometimes the outside wrapping can overshadow the contents.

Cooks can be gift-wrappers, too. Not necessarily to conceal but rather to dramatize a dish, to stimulate interest in and call attention to a culinary creation. The special "wrap" can take one of many forms—a savory, flaky piecrust tucked around a beef pie, fluffy dumplings rising from the surface of an aromatic chicken stew, a blanket of whipped potatoes covering a shepherd's pie. Who says a cook can't accomplish as much magic in the kitchen as the nimble-fingered lady at the department store gift-wrap counter? Except with the cook it's much more than surface illusion. Her "gift wraps" are meant to be eaten and enjoyed as well as eyed with delight.

Topping a stew with a piecrust immediately puts it in a very special category. It's no longer plain stew—it becomes a potpie and acquires a whole new character. Most men get very sentimental when confronted by a steaming savory potpie. Apparently, it evokes tender memories of childhood and mother in the kitchen. A friend of ours used to steel herself every time she attempted to serve her husband potpie. None of her efforts could compare with the potpies his mother made. He would rhapsodize about the homemade crust that would melt in the mouth. Finally, our friend asked her mother-in-law for the old family piecrust recipe. "I don't know what Dave is talking about," the dear lady said. "I never made piecrust in my life. I used to buy little potpies at the delicatessen and heat them up. I never dreamed Dave thought I made them!"

Which only proves how flaky piecrust can make the most level-headed man irrational.

For the cook who considers assembling a satisfactory stew challenge enough, there's no need to wrestle with a start-from-scratch piecrust recipe. You can save time and effort by using one of the instant piecrusts in the frozen foods section of your market. Or if you're a trifle more daring, try a packaged piecrust. It's practically foolproof as long as you follow the directions. And since you do have to roll the crust out on a floured board and tuck it around the stew, you can quite honestly answer in the affirmative when some inquiring guest asks, "Did *you* make this marvelous crust?"

Another toothsome, eye-catching covering that will win you oohs and ahs at the dinner table is the dumpling. Dumplings may have been a Chinese invention—they are mentioned in the earliest recorded annals of that country—but they really came into their own in Germany, centuries later. The Germans have always given dumplings star billing, based on their theory that anything edible will taste better with a dumpling. Accordingly, they drop, roll, and slide them into everything from soups to pies, and ragouts to fruit desserts.

Don't ever underrate dumplings; they are marvelous extenders and can help make a little go a long way. And they're not particular about the way you cook them—you can simmer, steam, bake, or fry dumplings. The important thing is to keep a weather eye on them while they cook. This can be tricky, so we suggest a period of experimentation for the beginner. There are certain basic rules that will guarantee success.

First, drop your dumpling mixture by the spoonful into hot, not lukewarm, liquid. For example, if dropping dumplings into soup, bring the soup to a boil, drop the dumplings by tablespoonfuls into the liquid so they don't touch, turn the heat to simmer, cover tightly, and simmer gently for 20 minutes. *Don't* lift the lid. Dumplings are shy and hate to be peeked at. If you're the type who can't stand suspense, try using a glass cover on your stew pan. That way you can watch your dumplings fatten and cook to your heart's content.

Keeping your dumplings apart when dropping them into the liquid helps them turn out light and fluffy. Always make certain there is plenty of gravy for them to cook in, as in the case of stew. If there are too many vegetables or too much meat on the surface, the dumplings won't have the hot surface they need to cook thoroughly. So, whatever you do, don't crowd them out with other ingredients.

Soggy dumplings are unpleasant to taste; make sure they are completely cooked through. Tip them up from the bottom and check. If they are still a little sticky underneath, continue simmering them for at least 5 more minutes.

It's only fair to tell you there's a school of thought that says dumplings should be cooked about 10 minutes covered, then uncovered and cooked 10 minutes more, or until they are nicely browned. If you like your dumplings to have a toasted look, then by all means make them this way.

Once you've mastered the art of cooking dumplings, you may want to experiment further and make, for example, cornmeal dumplings, a delicious accompaniment for chicken stew or ham hocks. Flavor them with nutmeg for chicken stew or use bacon drippings as the fat ingredient for dumplings in an Irish stew. Vary their taste by adding a teaspoon of celery seed or grated onion or two teaspoons of chopped parsley or chives to the dry ingredients. A quarter cup of shredded sharp cheese folded into the flour mixture will give you cheese dumplings.

If the members of your family are avid dumpling eaters and you don't have enough room in the pot for all they can devour, double the recipe and bake the extras on a lightly greased pan in the oven. And remember there's no law that says dumplings always have to be round; try cutting them in squares or strips, or use a cookie cutter and make fancy shapes for fancy occasions.

A great many one-dish meals can be enhanced by a snowy blanket of mashed potatoes or a crisp arrangement of biscuits. In each case, using an instant mashed potato mix or a can of refrigerator biscuits will be a time-saver. If you have a streak of the artist in you, you may want to use a pastry bag to swirl on your potato crust, but this isn't absolutely necessary. You can accomplish a very good-looking swirl with just a flourish of a tablespoon.

Chicken Paprikash with Dumplings

1 (4-pound size) ready-to-cook roasting chicken, cut up	6 tablespoons salad oil
3 tablespoons flour	2 tablespoons paprika
2¼ teaspoons salt	3 large onions, sliced (3 cups)
¼ teaspoon pepper	1 can (10½ ounces) condensed chicken broth, undiluted
	8 small carrots, pared

Dumplings

2 cups packaged biscuit mix	1 cup dairy sour cream
¼ teaspoon salt	1 tablespoon chopped parsley
¾ cup milk	

1. Wash chicken; pat dry with paper towels.

2. On waxed paper, combine flour, 2¼ teaspoons salt, and the pepper; use to coat chicken well. Reserve remaining flour mixture.

3. In 4 tablespoons hot oil in 6-quart Dutch oven, brown chicken, a few pieces at a time; remove as they are browned.

4. Add remaining oil to pan; stir in paprika. Add onion, and sauté until tender—about 5 minutes. Stir in reserved flour mixture until well blended. Gradually stir in chicken broth; bring to boiling, stirring.

5. Add browned chicken and carrots. Simmer, covered, 45 minutes, or until chicken is tender.

6. Meanwhile, make Dumplings: In medium-size bowl, combine biscuit mix, salt, and milk. Mix with fork until well blended.

7. Drop batter by rounded tablespoonfuls on boiling stew; cook over low heat, uncovered, 10 minutes. Cover tightly, and cook 10 to 15 minutes longer.

8. Carefully remove dumplings. Gradually stir sour cream into

chicken gravy; heat, but do not boil. Spoon chicken and gravy onto platter. Top with dumplings, and garnish with parsley.
Makes 4 to 6 servings.

Braised Short Ribs with Parsley Dumplings

5 pounds short ribs, in serving-size pieces	3 whole allspice
1 cup coarsely chopped onion	¼ teaspoon dried thyme leaves
2 teaspoons salt	1 can (10½ ounces) condensed beef bouillon, undiluted
¼ teaspoon pepper	1½ pounds carrots, pared and halved crosswise
1 bay leaf	

Dumplings

1 egg, slightly beaten	¼ cup chopped parsley
½ cup milk	
2 cups packaged biscuit mix	Parsley sprigs

1. Wipe short ribs with damp paper towels.

2. Slowly heat 6-quart Dutch oven. Add short ribs, fat side down; brown slowly on all sides—about 30 minutes in all. Pour off fat.

3. Add onion, salt, pepper, bay leaf, allspice, thyme, bouillon, and 2 cups water; bring to boiling.

4. Reduce heat; simmer, covered and stirring occasionally, 1½ hours—until tender. With spoon, skim off fat. Add carrots; simmer 30 minutes, or until carrots are fork-tender.

5. Meanwhile, make Dumplings: In medium-size bowl, combine egg and milk. Add biscuit mix and chopped parsley; stir until blended.

6. Drop batter by rounded tablespoonfuls into gently boiling liquid in Dutch oven. Cook over low heat, uncovered, 10 minutes. Cover tightly; cook 10 minutes longer.

7. Remove dumplings, short ribs, and carrots to heated serving platter. Spoon on pan juices, skimming off fat if necessary. Or, if desired, thicken juices: Measure liquid; return to pan. For each cup of liquid, stir 2 tablespoons flour with ¼ cup water until smooth; add to liquid. Bring to boiling, stirring; reduce heat, and simmer 5 minutes.

8. Garnish with parsley sprigs.
Makes 7 to 8 servings.

Veal Fricassee with Chive Dumplings

¼ cup unsifted all-purpose flour
1 teaspoon seasoned salt
⅛ teaspoon pepper
1 teaspoon dried thyme leaves
½ teaspoon poultry seasoning
2 pounds boneless shoulder of
   veal, cut into 1½-inch cubes
3 tablespoons salad oil
1 cup sliced onion
½ cup sliced celery

1 can (10½ ounces) chicken
   broth, undiluted
1 cup white wine
1 package (9 ounces) frozen
   Italian green beans
1 can (6 ounces) sliced
   mushrooms, undrained
3 tablespoons diced pimiento

Chive Dumplings (see below)

1. On sheet of waxed paper, combine flour, seasoned salt, pepper, thyme, and poultry seasoning; mix well. Roll veal cubes in flour mixture to coat well.

2. In hot oil in 4-quart Dutch oven, brown veal well, turning on all sides—takes about 20 minutes in all. Remove meat; set aside.

3. Add onion and celery to Dutch oven; sauté, stirring, about 5 minutes.

4. Return meat to Dutch oven. Add chicken broth and wine; stir to dissolve browned bits in Dutch oven.

5. Bring to boiling, over medium heat. Reduce heat; simmer, covered, about 1 hour, or till meat is tender.

6. Add frozen beans, undrained mushrooms, and pimiento; bring to boiling. Reduce heat, and cook, covered, 5 minutes.

7. Meanwhile, make Chive Dumplings. Bring stew just to boiling. Drop dumplings by heaping teaspoonfuls onto simmering stew. Cook, as directed under Chive Dumplings.

Makes 6 servings.

Chive Dumplings

1½ cups sifted all-purpose flour
2 teaspoons baking powder
½ teaspoon seasoned salt
2 tablespoons chopped chives

1 tablespoon butter or
   margarine, melted
1 egg, beaten
⅓ to ½ cup milk

1. Into medium-size bowl, sift flour, baking powder, and seasoned salt. Stir in chives.

2. With fork, stir in butter and egg; then stir in ⅓ cup milk. (If mixture seems dry, add a little more milk.)

3. Drop dumplings on simmering Veal Fricassee. Cook, tightly covered (do not lift lid), 25 minutes, or until dumplings are light and thoroughly cooked.

Makes about 18 dumplings.

Hash-Cheese Biscuit Bake

2 cans (15½-ounce size) corned-beef hash
⅛ teaspoon pepper
1½ cups grated sharp Cheddar cheese (about ⅓ pound)

1 package (8 ounces) refrigerator biscuits
1 tablespoon butter or margarine, melted
2 tablespoons finely chopped parsley

1. Preheat oven to 375° F.

2. In medium-size bowl, combine hash, pepper, and 1 cup grated cheese; mix well. Spread in layer in bottom of 10- by 6- by 2-inch baking dish. Sprinkle with ¼ cup grated cheese.

3. Bake, uncovered, 30 minutes.

4. Increase oven temperature to 475° F., or as package label on biscuits directs.

5. Separate biscuits. Dip top of each into melted butter, then into parsley combined with rest of cheese. Arrange biscuits, cheese side up, over top of hash.

6. Bake 10 minutes, or until biscuits are golden brown.

Makes 6 servings.

Ham-and-Asparagus Casserole with Biscuits

1 package (10 ounces) frozen cut asparagus spears
1 can (10½ ounces) condensed cream of celery soup
⅓ cup milk

1 cup grated sharp Cheddar cheese (¼ pound)
1 tablespoon chopped parsley
2 cans (4½-ounce size) deviled ham
4 hard-cooked eggs, sliced

Biscuit Topping

1 cup packaged biscuit mix	⅓ cup milk
1 tablespoon chopped parsley	

1. Cook asparagus as package label directs; drain.
2. Meanwhile, preheat oven to 450° F.
3. In medium-size saucepan, combine soup with milk; heat almost to boiling. Stir in cheese and parsley; keep hot.
4. In lightly buttered 2-quart casserole, layer asparagus, then ham, then eggs.
5. Make Biscuit Topping: In medium-size bowl, combine biscuit mix and parsley. With fork, stir in milk all at once. Dough will be soft.
6. Turn out dough onto lightly floured surface. Knead gently 8 to 10 times. Roll out to form a round 1 inch larger in diameter than casserole top.
7. Pour hot soup over casserole. Gently set biscuit top in place; make 3 slits in center.
8. Bake 10 to 15 minutes, or until golden.

Makes 4 to 6 servings.

Country Supper with Biscuits

1 pound ground chuck	1¾ cups fresh corn kernels, cut from cob
½ cup sliced red onion	
2 tablespoons flour	2 medium-size tomatoes, thinly sliced
1¾ teaspoons salt	
¼ teaspoon pepper	2 teaspoons sugar
1 large green pepper, cut into thin rings	¾ teaspoon ground thyme
	¼ teaspoon paprika

Biscuit Topping

2 cups packaged biscuit mix	¾ cup milk
1 cup grated sharp Cheddar cheese	

1. Preheat oven to 375° F.
2. In large skillet, over high heat, sauté chuck, stirring, until browned. Add onion; sauté 3 minutes.
3. Remove from heat. Stir in flour, 1¼ teaspoons salt, ¼ teaspoon pepper, and ½ cup water; mix well.
4. Spoon about a third of beef mixture into a 2-quart casserole. Layer, in order, a third of the green-pepper rings, a third of the corn, and a third of the tomato slices.
5. Combine rest of salt with the sugar, thyme, and paprika. Sprinkle a third of this mixture over tomato slices. Repeat layering of ingredients twice.
6. Bake casserole, uncovered, 30 minutes.
7. About 5 minutes before end of baking time, make Biscuit Topping: In medium-size bowl, combine biscuit mix with cheese. Add milk; stir just until combined.
8. Remove casserole from oven. Increase oven temperature to 425° F.
9. Drop biscuit dough, by tablespoonfuls, around edge of casserole. Bake, uncovered, 15 minutes longer.

Makes 6 servings.

Easy Chicken and Biscuit Pie

¾ cup canned chicken broth
1 package (9 ounces) frozen small onions with cream sauce
1 tablespoon chopped parsley
⅛ teaspoon dried thyme leaves

Dash pepper
1 jar (14 ounces) boned chicken
1 can (1 pound) whole carrots, drained

Biscuit Topping

2 tablespoons butter or margarine
1 tablespoon chopped chives

2 teaspoons chopped parsley
1 can (8.6 ounces) refrigerator flaky biscuits

1. Preheat oven to 375° F.
2. Pour chicken broth into small saucepan. Add frozen onions; cook as package label directs. Remove from heat.
3. Stir in 1 tablespoon parsley, the thyme, and pepper. Turn into shallow 1½-quart baking dish. Add chicken and carrots; mix gently. Place in oven.
4. Make Biscuit Topping: Divide butter into 12 pieces; place a piece in each of 12 muffin-pan cups. Place in oven just until melted. Mix chives and parsley.
5. Place a biscuit in each muffin-pan cup; turn, to coat with butter. Sprinkle chive mixture over tops.
6. Bake, along with chicken mixture, 15 minutes, or until golden.
7. To serve: Remove biscuits from cups. Arrange around edge of chicken mixture. Serve immediately.

Makes 4 servings.

Chicken Pie

1 (3½-pound size) whole, ready-to-cook roasting chicken
½ cup butter or margarine
1 slice bacon, chopped
½ pound Italian sweet sausage, sliced
½ pound lamb kidneys, quartered and fat removed
1 onion, peeled
1 carrot, pared and quartered
2 stalks celery with leaves
2 parsley sprigs
1 bay leaf

¼ teaspoon dried thyme leaves
1¼ teaspoons salt
¼ teaspoon pepper
1½ cups finely chopped carrot
2 cups finely chopped onion
½ teaspoon sugar
3 pounds tomatoes, peeled and chopped
½ cup dry sherry
¼ cup dry white wine
3 tablespoons flour
1 package (9½ ounces) piecrust mix
1 egg yolk

1. Wash chicken (also neck, heart, and liver) in cold water; dry on paper towels. Tuck wings of chicken under body; fasten skin at neck, and close body cavity with skewers; tie legs together with string.

2. In ¼ cup hot butter in heavy, 4-quart Dutch oven, brown chicken slowly all over, turning with 2 wooden spoons to avoid breaking skin—takes about 15 minutes. When chicken is browned, remove from Dutch oven, and set aside.

3. In same Dutch oven, brown chicken neck, heart, and liver along with bacon, sausage, and kidneys, stirring occasionally—takes about 10 minutes.

4. Set chicken on top of bacon mixture; add whole onion, quartered carrot, the celery, parsley, bay leaf, thyme, ½ teaspoon salt, ⅛ teaspoon pepper, and 1 cup water. Bring to boiling; reduce heat, and simmer, covered, 45 minutes, or until chicken is tender. Remove from heat. Remove skewers and string.

5. Meanwhile, in ¼ cup hot butter in 3-quart saucepan, sauté chopped carrot and onion with sugar, stirring occasionally, 30 minutes, or until carrot is tender. Add tomato, ¾ teaspoon salt, ⅛ teaspoon pepper, ¼ cup dry sherry, and the dry white wine. Bring to boiling; reduce heat, and simmer, covered, 10 minutes.

6. Combine flour and remaining sherry; mix well. Stir into tomato mixture. Bring to boiling, stirring, until mixture thickens. Remove from heat.

7. Lift chicken with sausage, bacon, and kidneys to a 3-quart oval casserole. Pour hot tomato sauce over all.

8. Preheat oven to 400° F. Make piecrust for 9-inch pie as package label directs. On lightly floured pastry cloth, roll out pastry in an oval shape to fit top of casserole. Arrange pastry over chicken, letting it hang over edge of casserole. Trim edge of pastry, and fold under ½ inch all around. Using fork, crimp edge of pastry, to secure to outside of casserole. Cut a few vents for steam.

9. In small bowl, mix egg yolk with 1 tablespoon cold water; use to brush over pastry. With remaining pastry, cut out 5 pastry leaves in the shape of bay leaves. Brush leaves with egg mixture; arrange on pastry, using egg mixture to fasten. Bake 20 to 25 minutes, or until crust is golden brown.

Makes 4 to 6 servings.

Holiday Squab Pie

Pastry

1 package piecrust mix	1 teaspoon salt
¼ teaspoon baking powder	½ teaspoon dried thyme leaves
3 tablespoons butter or regular margarine, softened	⅛ teaspoon pepper
	1½ cups Burgundy
4 squabs, halved (4 pounds in all), with livers	1 can (10½ ounces) condensed chicken broth, undiluted
⅓ cup butter or margarine	1 tablespoon currant jelly
12 small white onions, peeled	¾ teaspoon liquid gravy seasoning
½ cup cognac	¼ cup finely chopped carrot
1 cup diced fully cooked ham	1 egg yolk
½ cup flour	

1. Make Pastry: Prepare piecrust mix as package label directs, thoroughly blending baking powder with dry mix before adding water. Shape into a ball.

2. On lightly floured surface, roll out pastry to a 14- by 12-inch rectangle. At one end, spread 3 tablespoons butter over two-thirds of pastry, leaving ½-inch margin. Fold pastry in thirds, starting with unbuttered end.

3. With folded edge at right, carefully roll again to a 14- by 12-inch rectangle. (If butter breaks through, brush spot lightly with flour.) Fold in thirds, and wrap in waxed paper. Refrigerate until ready to use.

4. Singe squabs; wash; pat dry with paper towels. Chop livers; set aside.

5. In hot butter in large skillet or Dutch oven, brown onions. Remove, and set aside.

6. Brown squabs, a few halves at a time, on all sides in drippings in skillet. Remove as browned. Return all squabs to pan. Remove from heat.

7. Pour cognac over all, and ignite. When flame dies out, return to heat, and cook, covered, over low heat 10 minutes. Add onions and ham; cook 5 minutes longer. With slotted utensil, remove squabs, onions, and ham to a 2½-quart deep baking dish (about 12 by 10 inches); set aside.

8. Remove skillet from heat. Stir flour, salt, thyme, and pepper into drippings until well blended. Stir in Burgundy, chicken broth, jelly, and gravy seasoning.

9. Bring to boiling, stirring constantly. Boil 1 minute. Stir in the chopped liver and carrot. Pour over squab mixture in baking dish.

10. Preheat oven to 425° F.

11. On lightly floured surface, roll out pastry into a 14- by 12-inch rectangle. Trim edges (save trimmings to make pastry decorations).

12. Fold pastry rectangle in half lengthwise. Unfold over filled baking dish; cut several slits for steam vents; crimp edge. Roll out trimmings, and cut as desired.

13. Beat egg yolk with 1 teaspoon water. Brush over pastry. (If using pastry decorations, gently press in place. Save some of egg mixture to brush over decorations.)

14. Bake 10 minutes. Reduce oven temperature to 350° F.; bake 1¼ hours longer. If pastry becomes too brown, cover loosely with foil.

Makes 4 to 6 servings.

Beef-and-Vegetable Potpie

3	pounds boneless beef chuck	1	teaspoon Worcestershire sauce
2	tablespoons salad oil		
1	clove garlic, crushed	12	small white onions, peeled
1	can (10½ ounces) condensed beef consommé, undiluted	1	pound carrots, pared
		4	medium-size potatoes, pared
1	can (8 ounces) tomato sauce with onion	1	cup frozen green peas
		1	can (8 ounces) whole green beans, drained
2	teaspoons salt		
½	teaspoon dried thyme leaves	½	cup flour
6	whole black peppercorns	1	package (9.5 ounces) refrigerator flaky biscuits
1	bay leaf		
		1	egg yolk

1. Wipe beef with damp paper towels. Cut into 1-inch cubes, discarding excess fat.

2. In hot oil in 6-quart Dutch oven or heavy kettle, over medium heat, brown one-third of beef cubes at a time until browned on all sides. Remove as browned.

3. Add garlic; sauté 1 minute. Return all beef to pan. Add consommé, tomato sauce, salt, thyme, peppercorns, bay leaf, Worcestershire, and 1⅓ cups water.

4. Bring to boiling; reduce heat, and simmer, covered, 1 hour. Add whole onions; simmer 30 minutes longer.

5. Meanwhile, cut carrots in 1-inch pieces; cut potatoes in 1-inch cubes. Add to meat mixture; simmer 30 minutes longer, or until vegetables are tender. Add frozen peas and drained beans; cook 5 minutes longer.

6. Preheat oven to 400° F.

7. With slotted spoon, remove meat and vegetables to a 3-quart casserole. Strain liquid into a 4-cup measure; skim off fat, and discard. You should have 2 cups liquid left. (Add water if needed.) Return liquid to Dutch oven.

8. In small bowl, blend flour with 1 cup water until smooth. Stir into liquid; bring to boiling over medium heat, stirring constantly until gravy thickens. Pour over meat and vegetables in casserole. Place in oven; bake 25 minutes.

9. Meanwhile, remove biscuits from package. Roll out one biscuit; use palms of hands to make a 10-inch-long strip. Repeat, to make 7 strips in all. Place strips, lattice fashion, on ungreased cookie sheet. Place remaining 3 biscuits alongside.

10. Beat egg yolk and 1 tablespoon water together with a fork. Brush strips with egg-yolk mixture.

11. Bake 15 minutes, or until biscuit strips are golden brown.

12. To serve: Place biscuit lattice on top of casserole.

Makes 8 servings.

Golden Beef-Potato Pie

1 cup evaporated milk, undiluted	2 teaspoons dry mustard
½ cup canned tomato puree	¾ teaspoon pepper
1¾ cups raw quick-cooking oats	½ teaspoon dried thyme leaves
3 eggs	⅔ cup finely chopped onion
1 tablespoon salt	3 pounds ground chuck

Potato Topping

1   package (11 ounces), or 2
    packages (7-ounce size),
    instant mashed potatoes
Milk
Butter or margarine
Salt
Pepper

¼ cup butter or margarine,
    melted
⅓ cup grated Parmesan cheese

Creole Sauce (see below)

1. Preheat oven to 350° F.
2. In large bowl, combine milk, tomato puree, and oats, mixing well. Add eggs, salt, mustard, pepper, thyme, and onion, mixing well.
3. Add chuck, stirring lightly with fork until thoroughly combined. Turn into a 15½- by 10½- by 2¼-inch baking pan, spreading evenly; bake 30 minutes.
4. Meanwhile, prepare mashed potatoes as package label directs, using amounts of milk, butter, salt, and pepper called for on label.
5. Swirl potatoes over meat; brush top with ¼ cup melted butter, and sprinkle with cheese. Bake 20 minutes. Then, if desired, run under broiler, 4 inches from heat, until golden—about 1 minute.
6. To serve, cut into 12 squares. Serve topped with Creole Sauce.
Makes 12 servings.

Creole Sauce

1   can (1 pound) stewed
    tomatoes
1   tablespoon chopped parsley
¼ cup finely chopped green
    pepper

¼ teaspoon salt
⅛ teaspoon pepper
1   bay leaf
1   tablespoon cornstarch

1. Crush large pieces of tomato with back of spoon. Combine with rest of ingredients, except cornstarch, in small saucepan; bring to boiling, stirring.
2. Reduce heat; simmer, uncovered, 15 minutes. Remove bay leaf, and discard.

3. Meanwhile, in small bowl, combine cornstarch and 2 teaspoons water, making a smooth paste.

4. Stir into tomato mixture; bring to boiling, stirring. Mixture will be slightly thickened, and translucent.

Makes 2¼ cups—enough for 12 servings.

Hamburger Hot Pot

1½ pound ground chuck
1 clove garlic, crushed
1 teaspoon salt
⅛ teaspoon pepper
6 medium-size potatoes (2 pounds), pared, cut into ¼-inch-thick slices

3 medium-size onions, sliced (2 cups)
1 can (10½ ounces) condensed golden-mushroom soup, undiluted

Chopped parsley
Catsup

1. Preheat oven to 350° F.

2. Heat a large skillet. Add chuck, and sauté, stirring with fork, until brown—about 10 minutes. Pour off fat. Stir in garlic, ½ teaspoon salt, and the pepper.

3. In 2½-quart casserole, place half the potato slices, then half the onion; add the browned meat; top with remaining potato and onion. Sprinkle with ½ teaspoon salt. Add soup, spreading evenly over all.

4. Bake, covered, 1½ hours. Garnish with parsley. Serve with catsup. Makes 6 servings.

Parmesan Shepherd's Pie

1½ pounds baking potatoes, peeled and cut into quarters (about 3½ to 4 cups)
8 tablespoons butter, softened
⅓ to ½ cup heavy cream
Salt
Freshly ground black pepper
⅓ cup finely chopped onions

¼ teaspoon finely chopped garlic
3 tablespoons flour
1½ cups braising liquid from the braised lamb, or an equivalent amount of fresh or canned beef stock, or a combination of both

1 teaspoon tomato paste	1 tablespoon finely chopped
1 tablespoon red-wine vinegar	parsley
2 cups (packed down) braised lamb, chopped and trimmed of all fat and gristle	¼ cup Parmesan cheese, freshly grated, mixed with 2 tablespoons dry bread crumbs

1. Cook the quartered potatoes in salted boiling water to cover until they are tender but not falling apart. Drain them at once; return them to the pan, and shake them over low heat until they are dry and mealy.

2. Force the potatoes through a ricer, and beat into them, either by hand or with an electric mixer, 4 tablespoons of softened butter and then the cream, a few tablespoons at a time. Use as much cream as you need to make the puree smooth; but make sure it remains thick enough to hold its shape in a spoon. Season the potatoes with salt and freshly ground black pepper.

3. While the potatoes are cooking, melt 3 tablespoons of butter in a heavy frying pan. When the foam subsides, add the finely chopped onions. Cook over moderate heat for about 6 minutes, stirring frequently, until the onions are soft, transparent, and lightly colored. Then stir in the garlic, and cook a moment longer.

4. Remove from heat, add flour, and stir until smooth. Pour in 1½ cups of braising liquid or stock; beat vigorously with a whisk, to partially dissolve the flour. Then cook over moderate heat, whisking constantly, until the sauce becomes smooth and very thick.

5. Add the tomato paste and the vinegar, and simmer for 1 or 2 minutes before stirring in the chopped lamb. Mix the lamb and sauce thoroughly, and cook for 2 minutes, or until the meat absorbs some of the sauce. Taste for seasoning.

6. Preheat the oven to 400° F. Butter an 8-cup soufflé dish or deep baking dish attractive enough to take to the table. Spread about a cupful of the warm whipped potatoes on the bottom, smoothing it with a spatula. Carefully spoon the lamb mixture over the top. Sprinkle the meat with a tablespoon of chopped parsley. Now spread the remaining potatoes over the layer of meat, again smoothing it into place with a spatula.

7. Dust the top evenly with the Parmesan-crumb mixture, and dot all over with a tablespoon of butter.

8. Bake in the center of the hot oven for about 20 minutes, or until the top of the pie is lightly browned. Slide under the broiler for a few seconds, to give the crust a little more color, and serve at once.

Makes 6 servings.

Baked Lamb-Chop-and-Potato Hot Pot

6 shoulder lamb chops (about 3½ pounds)
¼ cup flour
2 teaspoons salt
½ teaspoon pepper
1 can (10½ ounces) condensed chicken broth, undiluted

2 teaspoons bottled steak sauce
1 pound onions, peeled and sliced
6 carrots, pared and sliced (½ pound)
6 potatoes, pared and sliced (1½ pounds)

1. Preheat oven to 350° F. Trim excess fat from lamb chops. Heat trimmed fat in large, heavy skillet.

2. On waxed paper, combine flour, salt, and pepper. Dip chops in flour mixture, coating lightly. Reserve remaining flour mixture.

3. In hot fat, brown chops on both sides. Remove from heat. Remove chops from skillet.

4. Stir reserved flour mixture into 2 tablespoons drippings in skillet until smooth. Gradually stir in chicken broth and steak sauce; bring to boiling, stirring constantly. Reduce heat; simmer 1 minute. Remove from heat.

5. In 3½-quart casserole, layer half of onion and carrot; cover with browned chops. Add half of potato and the remaining onion. Overlap remaining potato and carrot slices over top. Pour broth mixture over all.

6. Bake, covered, 2 hours. Uncover, and bake 30 minutes longer, or until meat and potatoes are tender.

Makes 6 servings.

Lamb Hot Pot

2 pounds small white potatoes, pared

2 pounds lamb shoulder cut into 1½-inch cubes

1 large onion, sliced
2 cups sliced carrots (about 5)
2 teaspoons salt
½ teaspoon pepper
1 cup canned chicken broth

2 tablespoons butter or
margarine, melted
1 can (10¾ ounces) chicken
gravy

1. Preheat oven to 350° F. Grease well a 3-quart Dutch oven.

2. Slice potatoes ¼ inch thick. Layer half in prepared Dutch oven. Cover with lamb, then sliced onion and carrots. Sprinkle with salt and pepper.

3. Place remaining potato slices, overlapping, on carrots. Pour broth over all.

4. Brush tops of potato slices with butter; bake, covered, 2 hours.

5. Bake, uncovered, about 50 minutes more, or until potatoes are crisp and browned.

6. Meanwhile, heat gravy over low heat. Pour gravy around edge of Dutch oven.

Makes 4 servings.

Veal Potpie

2 tablespoons salad oil
3 pounds boneless veal, cut into
3-inch cubes

2 teaspoons salt
¼ teaspoon pepper
3½ cups boiling water

Dumpling Squares

1½ cups sifted all-purpose flour
½ teaspoon salt
1 teaspoon baking powder
1½ tablespoons butter or
margarine
1 egg, beaten

1 large onion, coarsely chopped
(¾ cup)
3 cups pared, diced potatoes (1
pound)
3 tablespoons chopped parsley
1 teaspoon paprika

1. In hot oil in 4½- to 5-quart Dutch oven, brown veal well, turning on all sides—15 to 20 minutes in all. Sprinkle with salt and pepper.

2. Add boiling water; bring to boiling. Reduce heat, and simmer, covered, 45 minutes, or until veal is almost tender.

3. Meanwhile, make Dumpling Squares: Sift flour with salt and baking powder into medium-size bowl. With pastry blender or 2 knives, cut in butter until particles are size of large peas.

4. With fork, quickly stir in egg and 3 to 4 tablespoons cold water. (Dough will be rather stiff, but should clean side of bowl.)

5. On lightly floured surface, roll out dough ⅛ inch thick, to form a rectangle 12 by 6 inches.

6. With sharp knife, cut dough into 1½-inch squares. Let stand, uncovered, several minutes.

7. Meanwhile, to veal in Dutch oven, add onion, potato, 2 tablespoons parsley, and the paprika. Simmer, covered, 10 minutes.

8. Remove cover; drop half of dumpling squares, one by one, into simmering liquid. As they drop to the bottom, add remaining squares, stirring in carefully.

9. Simmer, covered, 25 minutes, or until dumplings are light and cooked through. Sprinkle top with remaining parsley.

Makes 6 to 8 servings.

Pork Potpie

1 pound pork shoulder, cut into ½-inch cubes	½ package (10-ounce size) frozen peas and carrots
1 chicken-bouillon cube, dissolved in 1 cup boiling water	1 can (8 ounces) small white potatoes, drained
1 teaspoon vinegar	1 can (8 ounces) small white onions, drained
1 teaspoon salt	1½ tablespoons flour
⅛ teaspoon pepper	½ package (10-ounce size) piecrust mix
¼ teaspoon sage	¼ teaspoon poultry seasoning
1 bay leaf	
1 clove garlic	

1. In large saucepan, over high heat, brown pork cubes, on all sides—about 5 minutes.

2. Reduce heat. Add bouillon, vinegar, salt, pepper, sage, bay leaf, and garlic; simmer, covered, 30 minutes.

3. Add peas and carrots, potatoes, and onions; simmer, covered, 15 minutes. Remove garlic; discard.

4. Meanwhile, in small bowl, blend flour with ¼ cup water to make a smooth paste. Add to stew; bring to boiling, stirring. Boil 2 minutes, to thicken stew slightly.

5. Ladle stew into 4 (10-ounce size) individual casseroles.

6. Preheat oven to 425° F.

7. Make piecrust as package label directs, adding poultry seasoning to dry ingredients.

8. On lightly floured surface, roll pastry into an 11-inch square. Cut into four 4¾-inch circles. Adjust a pastry circle over each casserole; then flute the edge. Make several small slits in center of pastry, for steam vents.

9. Bake 20 minutes, or until pastry is golden brown.

Makes 4 servings.

Cheese, Leek, and Ham Pie

1 package (1⅞ ounces) dry cream of leek soup mix
2 cups milk
1 cup light cream
4 eggs
2½ cups grated natural Swiss cheese (½ pound)
1 teaspoon dry mustard
1 teaspoon salt
¼ teaspoon pepper
2 cans (4½-ounce size) deviled ham
3 tablespoons packaged dry bread crumbs
1 (10-inch) prepared pie shell

1. In medium-size saucepan, with wooden spoon, blend soup mix with milk.

2. Over medium heat, bring to boiling, stirring. Remove from heat; cool slightly. Stir in cream. Refrigerate until cold—20 minutes.

3. Meanwhile, preheat oven to 375° F.

4. With rotary beater, beat eggs in large bowl with soup mixture. Mix in cheese, mustard, salt, and pepper.

5. Mix deviled ham with bread crumbs.

6. Spread ham mixture evenly in bottom of pie shell. Pour in filling.

7. Bake 50 minutes, or until set—when a sharp knife inserted in the center comes out clean. Cool pie slightly before serving.

Makes 8 servings.

Corned-Beef-and-Potato Pie

1 can (3 ounces) chopped
  mushrooms
1 can (12 ounces) corned beef,
  cubed
1 can (1 pound, 1 ounce) red
  kidney beans, undrained
½ cup chili sauce
2 teaspoons Worcestershire
  sauce

½ package (5⅝ -ounce size)
  instant mashed potatoes
½ cup milk
½ teaspoon salt
Dash pepper
2 tablespoons butter or
  margarine

1. Drain mushrooms, reserving the liquid.

2. In medium-size saucepan, combine corned beef, kidney beans, mushrooms, chili sauce, and Worcestershire; mix well. Bring to boiling; reduce heat, and simmer, covered, stirring occasionally, 5 minutes.

3. Add water to mushroom liquid to measure 1½ cups. Prepare potatoes as package label directs, using mushroom liquid, milk, salt, pepper, and butter. Beat potato mixture, with fork, until light and fluffy.

4. Turn corned-beef mixture into a 1½-quart casserole. Swirl potatoes in mounds around edge of casserole.

5. Run under broiler, uncovered, 3 inches from heat, 8 to 10 minutes, or until potatoes are golden.

Makes 4 to 6 servings.

VII

Quick and Easy Combinations

❀ ❀ ❀

If you're a slowpoke in the kitchen certain one-dish meals can change your whole image.

In fact, it's entirely possible you'll spend more time looking for your potholder than you will assembling these meals, because they're designed to be put together in a gratifying flash.

The gratification comes not so much when you're enjoying the meal but when your husband says, "I don't know how you do it! You got home from the hairdresser's five minutes later than I got home from the office. As far as I could see, nothing was started in the kitchen, yet you still got dinner on the table within a half hour!"

Collect such compliments without explanations. It's every cook's privilege to cherish her own little secrets and, in this instance, the secret involves such reliable assets as a can opener and cans. Plus imagination, which doesn't come in cans.

Mothers-in-law are inclined to scoff at the idea, but there's nothing wrong in creating a meal entirely from convenience foods. Naturally, there'll be days when you will want to start from scratch: clean and

177

peel the vegetables, sear and season the meat, and mix and roll the piecrust. But when you are faced with an emergency or when time is of the essence, reach for the recipes in this chapter. They can be lifesavers.

These are recipes that take full advantage of canned foods—canned soups, canned corned beef or hash, canned tomatoes, pork and beans, and sauerkraut, to mention a few. Frankfurters, ground meat, and spaghetti also play starring roles in many of these speedy one-dish choices. All are not only simple to prepare but economical as well. In fact, a good friend always refers inversely to the Saturday-Night Bean Bake as her favorite "thrift-spend" meal. Her twelve-year-old son has the explanation. "Thrift-spend just means we're saving on food bills so we can splurge on a family camper," he says.

There are many small ways in which you can save time when preparing a meal, even one labeled quick and easy. Here are a few:

Measure dry ingredients first, put them on waxed paper, then use the same cup for liquids or fats. This saves washing the measuring cup for re-use.

For easy measuring of solid fats, have them at room temperature, not rock-hard from the refrigerator so that you have to wrestle them into cup or spoon.

Preheat your oven while you are preparing the dish to be baked or preheat the surface pan you are going to use with hot water.

Have a container of presifted flour ready. When you bring home a bag of flour, sift half of it and keep it in a separate container.

Keep kitchen shears on hand and use them to cut up vegetables and garnishes quickly, as well as to cube meat and cut slices of cooked chicken or turkey into small pieces.

Even though you're in a mad rush, be careful with seasonings. A wild splatter of salt could ruin your meal. Salt vegetables just before removing from the heat. Salt meat for use in soup stock or stew just before cooking so the meat juices will flavor the broth or gravy. Meats like hamburger patties may be salted before, during, or after cooking, although purists suggest afterward, in order to keep meat juices locked in during cooking. And don't directly salt vegetables in salads; instead, use the salt in the dressing.

Run frozen vegetable blocks under warm water so they will separate quickly when dropped into boiling water.

Snap spaghetti into thirds before dropping into boiling water; it will save time in stirring. (And eating—no chasing long strands around the plate.) A tablespoon of butter or cooking oil in the water will keep the spaghetti from boiling over.

If your recipe calls for more than one canned item, open all cans at the same time to eliminate several trips to the can opener.

Keep your emergency meal ingredients together on one shelf so you won't have to hunt high and low for some missing item when an emergency arises. As soon as you use any item, replace it on your very next shopping trip.

If you're preparing a casserole or stew, be sure to use an attractive stove-to-table container to avoid having to transfer the food from pot to serving dish at mealtime.

One warning, though: don't overdo the dispatch with which you turn out these quickie casseroles. Avoid the temptation to serve them in a kind of slapdash manner. That can be a serious mistake. The time-saver, economy meal deserves as much "window-dressing" as the lavish company menu. Put out your prettiest stoneware, the place mats from that little Mexican gift shop, the cranberry water goblets, and flowers on the table—it's this kind of setting that will make your minor culinary effort look like a masterpiece in the eyes of the beholder. And it may even taste better.

Family Supper Casserole

1 package (8 ounces) thin spaghetti	¼ teaspoon salt
	⅛ teaspoon pepper
1 pound ground beef chuck	1½ cups grated sharp Cheddar cheese (6 ounces)
¾ cup chili sauce	
1 teaspoon dried oregano leaves	1½ cups milk

1. Cook spaghetti as package label directs. Drain.

2. Preheat oven to 350° F.

3. In large skillet, sauté chuck until no longer red. Drain. Stir in ½ cup chili sauce, the oregano, salt, and pepper.

4. In well-greased 2-quart casserole, place half of spaghetti, then half of meat mixture; sprinkle with half of cheese. Add remaining spaghetti,

meat, and cheese. Pour milk over all. Top with remaining ¼ cup chili sauce.

5. Bake, uncovered, 35 minutes, or until milk is absorbed and cheese is melted.

Makes 6 servings.

Beef Balls on Skewers

1 pound ground chuck	3 large green peppers
1 can (4½ ounces) deviled ham	25 cherry tomatoes
3 ounces Roquefort or blue cheese	Salt
	Pepper

1. In medium-size bowl, combine chuck and deviled ham; mix lightly with fork.

2. Cut cheese into 25 cubes. Cut green peppers into 2- by 1-inch pieces.

3. Shape the meat mixture around cheese cubes, to form 25 meatballs.

4. On each of 25 hibachi sticks, thread a meatball, a green-pepper piece, and a cherry tomato at end. Sprinkle lightly with salt and pepper. Refrigerate.

5. At serving time, broil, on hibachi or in broiler, about 5 minutes on each side, or until nicely browned. Cheese will be melted on inside.

Makes 25; 4 servings.

Corned-Beef-Hash and Vegetable Casserole

2 cans (15½-ounce size) corned-beef hash	⅛ teaspoon pepper
	1 can (10¾ ounces) beef gravy
1 can (1 pound) mixed vegetables, well drained	¾ cup canned French-fried onions

1. Preheat oven to 375° F.

2. In a 1½-quart casserole, break up hash with fork. Add vegetables, pepper, and ½ cup gravy; toss to mix well. Top the hash mixture with onions.

3. Bake the hash mixture, uncovered, 30 minutes, or until it is hot and bubbly.

4. To serve: Heat rest of gravy. Serve along with Corned-Beef-Hash and Vegetable Casserole.

Makes 6 servings.

Coin-Dot Casserole

¼ cup chopped onion
½ cup canned chopped mushrooms
½ teaspoon dried oregano leaves

2 cans (15½-ounce size) spaghetti and meatballs
¼ pound sharp Cheddar cheese

1. Preheat oven to 400° F. In medium-size bowl, combine onion, mushrooms, oregano, and spaghetti and meatballs. Toss lightly to mix well. Turn into a 10- by 6-inch baking dish.

2. Cut cheese into ¾-inch cubes. Sprinkle over top of casserole.

3. Bake 20 minutes, or until cheese is slightly melted and golden brown.

Makes 6 servings.

Quick Cassoulet

4 slices bacon, coarsely chopped
1 (2-pound size) broiler-fryer, cut up
6 Italian sweet sausages, or 6 brown-and-serve sausages
1½ cups chopped onion
1 clove garlic, finely chopped
½ cup chopped parsley

2 cans (8-ounce size) tomato sauce
1 cup dry white wine
1 teaspoon salt
½ teaspoon crushed black pepper
1 bay leaf
3 cans (20-ounce size) white kidney beans, drained

1. Preheat oven to 375° F.

2. In 5-quart, flameproof casserole or Dutch oven, cook bacon until crisp. Remove with slotted spoon; drain on paper towels.

3. In hot bacon drippings, brown chicken and sausages, turning to brown evenly. Remove to baking pan as they brown. Bake, uncovered, about 10 minutes.

4. Meanwhile, to remaining drippings in casserole, add onion, garlic, parsley; cook over medium heat till onion is golden—about 5 minutes.

5. Add tomato sauce, wine, salt, pepper, and bay leaf; bring to boiling. Reduce heat; add beans; mix well. Remove chicken and sausages from oven, and add to casserole. Sprinkle with bacon.

6. Bake, uncovered, 30 minutes, or until thoroughly tender.

Makes 6 to 8 servings.

Frankfurter Goulash

1½ pounds frankfurters	1 beef-bouillon cube
2 tablespoons butter or margarine	1 cup boiling water
2 cups chopped onion	1 can (1 pound, 11 ounces) sauerkraut, drained
1 clove garlic, finely chopped	2 cups dairy sour cream
1 tablespoon paprika	
1 teaspoon dried dill weed	**Boiled or mashed potatoes**
1 teaspoon caraway seed	**(optional)**

1. Cut frankfurters in half crosswise.

2. In hot butter in Dutch oven or heavy kettle, sauté onion, garlic, and paprika until onion is soft. Add frankfurters, dill, caraway, bouillon cube, and boiling water.

3. Bring to boiling; reduce heat, and simmer, covered, 15 minutes.

4. Add sauerkraut; simmer, covered, 15 minutes longer.

5. Stir in sour cream; heat but do not boil. Serve with boiled or mashed potatoes, if desired.

Makes 8 servings.

Frankfurter-and-Eggplant Supper

1 eggplant (1¼ pounds)	½ cup chopped onion
Flour	1½ teaspoons salt
⅓ cup olive or salad oil	¼ teaspoon pepper

¼ teaspoon dried basil leaves
1 small clove garlic, crushed
1 pound frankfurters, cut in
   1-inch pieces

1 can (1 pound) tomatoes,
   undrained

Cooked white rice

1. Peel eggplant; cut into 1-inch cubes. Measure 5 cups. Toss eggplant with flour to coat lightly.

2. In hot oil in large skillet, sauté onion until tender—about 5 minutes.

3. Add eggplant, salt, pepper, basil, and garlic; cook, stirring occasionally, until eggplant is lightly browned.

4. Add frankfurters and tomatoes, mixing well. Simmer, covered, 20 minutes, stirring occasionally. Serve over rice.

Makes 6 servings.

Pork-and-Potato Pie

1 piece (1½ pounds) cooked
   fresh-ham roll
1 can (1 pound, 4 ounces)
   apple slices, undrained
¼ cup cracker meal
¼ teaspoon dried sage leaves
1½ teaspoons salt
¼ teaspoon pepper

4 tablespoons butter or
   margarine
1 can (13¾ ounces) chicken
   broth
1 package (11 ounces) or 2
   packages (7-ounce size)
   instant mashed potatoes

1. Preheat oven to 400° F.

2. Cut ham roll into ½-inch cubes. Place in 8-inch round baking dish. Stir in apples, cracker meal, sage, salt, and pepper.

3. Dot top with 3 tablespoons butter. Add ¾ cup chicken broth. Cover baking dish with foil; bake 15 minutes.

4. Meanwhile, prepare mashed potatoes, as package label directs, substituting remaining 1 cup chicken broth for 1 cup water.

5. Remove foil from baking dish. Spoon potatoes over meat mixture, swirling top. Dot with 1 tablespoon butter.

6. Broil, 3 inches from heat, just until potatoes are golden brown—5 to 7 minutes.

Makes 6 servings.

Ham-and-Cabbage Casserole

2 teaspoons instant minced onion
1½ teaspoons salt
8 small whole unpared new potatoes
½ small head cabbage, cut into 4 wedges and cored
6 large carrots, pared and cut into 4-inch sticks
1 pound canned ham or corned beef
4 tablespoons butter or margarine
Frankfurter relish

1. Set electric skillet at 300° F., or place skillet over moderately high heat. In the skillet, bring 3 cups water to boiling; add onion and salt.
2. Add potatoes; cook, covered, 25 minutes, or until tender. (Add another ½ cup water during cooking, if necessary.)
3. Add cabbage and carrots; cook 10 minutes longer.
4. Place ham in center of skillet; dot vegetables with butter. Cover, and cook 5 minutes longer.
5. Serve right from skillet, along with relish.
Makes 4 servings.

Luncheon Meat Casserole

2 cans (1-pound size) pork and beans in tomato sauce
1 can (13½ ounces) pineapple chunks, drained
1 tablespoon instant minced onion
1 teaspoon dry mustard
1 can (12 ounces) luncheon meat
Whole cloves
2 tablespoons light-brown sugar

1. Preheat oven to 350° F.
2. Turn beans into 1½-quart baking dish. Gently stir in pineapple, onion, and mustard.
3. Cut luncheon meat into quarters lengthwise; then cut each piece in half crosswise, to make 3½- by ¾- by ¾-inch pieces. Score each, and arrange on beans to make stripes. Stud each piece of meat with 2 or 3 cloves, and sprinkle with brown sugar.
4. Bake, uncovered, 30 minutes, or until beans are bubbling.
Makes 4 to 6 servings.

Bean-and-Sausage Casserole

1 package (8 ounces) brown-and-serve sausages or sausage patties
1 can (1 pound) pork and beans
1 can (15 ounces) red kidney beans, drained

⅓ cup catsup
1 tablespoon prepared mustard
2 teaspoons Worcestershire sauce
2 corn toaster muffins, quartered

1. Preheat oven to 375° F.
2. Prepare sausages or patties as package label directs. Cut sausages into thirds or patties into chunks.
3. In a 1½-quart casserole, combine sausages, pork and beans, kidney beans, catsup, mustard, and Worcestershire; mix well.
4. Bake, covered, 20 minutes. Remove cover. Arrange muffins around edge of casserole; bake 10 minutes longer.
Makes 4 servings.

Sausage-and-Apple Scallop

2 large apples (about 1¼ pounds)
2 teaspoons lemon juice
1 pound frankfurters
3 tablespoons butter or margarine
2 medium-size onions, cut into ¼-inch-thick slices (about 1 cup)

1 can (6 ounces) apple juice
3 tablespoons brown sugar, firmly packed
½ teaspoon salt

Potato pancakes (optional)

1. Core apples, but do not peel; cut into ¼-inch-thick wedges. Sprinkle with lemon juice. Cut each frankfurter, on the diagonal, into thirds.
2. In hot butter in large skillet, sauté onion slices until golden and tender—about 5 minutes.
3. Add apple wedges, frankfurters, apple juice, brown sugar, and salt; stir gently. Simmer, covered, about 15 minutes, or until frankfurters are puffed and apple is tender.
4. Arrange on heated platter. Serve with potato pancakes, if desired.
Makes 4 to 6 servings.

Sausage-Macaroni Goulash

1 pound pork-sausage links	1 teaspoon salt
1 cup chopped green pepper	¼ teaspoon pepper
1 cup chopped onion	1 tablespoon bottled thick
1 can (1 pound, 12 ounces)	steak sau ʻe
tomatoes, undrained	1 cup dairy ʒour cream
1 cup uncooked elbow	
macaroni	Chopped parsley

1. Halve sausages crosswise. Sauté in large skillet until nicely browned. Remove.

2. Drain off all but 3 tablespoons fat from skillet. In hot fat, sauté green pepper and onion, stirring, about 5 minutes.

3. Add sausages, tomatoes, macaroni, salt, pepper, and steak sauce; bring to boiling. Reduce heat; simmer, covered, 30 minutes, stirring occasionally.

4. Remove from heat. Stir in sour cream, mixing well. Sprinkle with parsley.

Makes 4 servings.

Tongue-Hash Casserole

2 cups coarsely ground cooked	¼ cup mustard pickle,
tongue	undrained, coarsely chopped
1½ cups chopped cold cooked	2 tablespoons packaged
potatoes	seasoned dry bread crumbs
3 tablespoons chopped onion	1 teaspoon butter or margarine
⅛ teaspoon pepper	
	Parsley sprigs

1. Preheat oven to 375° F. Lightly grease a 1-quart casserole.

2. In medium-size bowl, toss the ground tongue with potatoes, onion, pepper, and mustard pickle to mix thoroughly.

3. Turn tongue mixture into prepared casserole. Combine bread crumbs and butter. Sprinkle over top of casserole.

4. Bake 35 minutes, or until bubbly and top is nicely browned. Garnish with parsley.

Makes 4 servings.

Sliced-Turkey-and-Broccoli Casserole

2 packages (10-ounce size) frozen broccoli spears with hollandaise sauce	12 slices cooked turkey (1½ pounds)
	1 cup dairy sour cream
	½ cup grated Cheddar cheese

1. Preheat oven to 450° F. Cook broccoli as package label directs; drain.
2. Meanwhile, wrap turkey in foil. Place in oven to heat through.
3. Thaw pouches of hollandaise sauce as directed. Add to sour cream and ¼ cup cheese in a small bowl; stir just until blended.
4. Arrange broccoli in shallow baking dish, 12 by 8 by 2 inches; top with turkey slices, overlapping slightly. Spoon sauce over all; sprinkle with remaining cheese.
5. Run under broiler until cheese is melted—about 2 minutes.
Makes 6 servings.

Turkey Curry

1 can (1 pound) fruits for salad	1 jar (7¾ ounces) apples and apricots
1 can (10½ ounces) condensed cream of chicken soup, undiluted	1 tablespoon butter or margarine
1¼ teaspoons curry powder	
1 can (1 pound, 14 ounces) fully cooked, boneless turkey	Prepared chutney

1. Preheat electric skillet to 350° F., or set skillet over moderately high heat.
2. Drain fruits for salad, reserving 2 tablespoons syrup.
3. In skillet, combine reserved syrup, chicken soup, 1 teaspoon curry powder, the liquid from can of turkey, and apples and apricots; stir to mix well. Bring mixture to boiling; then reduce heat.
4. Place turkey, in one piece, in sauce; spoon sauce over it. Heat, covered, 8 to 10 minutes, or until thoroughly hot.
5. Meanwhile, in small saucepan, combine butter, ¼ teaspoon curry powder, and the fruits for salad. Heat gently. Spoon the fruit mixture over and around turkey. Serve with chutney.
Makes 4 to 6 servings.

Curried Tuna-and-Potato Casserole

1 package (5.35 ounces)
scalloped potatoes
1½ to 2 teaspoons curry powder
2 tablespoons butter or
margarine
2 cups boiling water
⅔ cup milk

2 cans (7-ounce size)
chunk-style tuna, well
drained and flaked
¼ cup chopped, drained
prepared chutney

¼ cup salted-peanut halves
1 small tomato, sliced

1. Preheat oven to 400° F.
2. In 1½-quart casserole, combine potatoes with seasonings from package and curry powder according to taste.
3. Stir in butter, boiling water, milk, tuna, and chutney.
4. Bake, uncovered, for 30 to 35 minutes, or until the potatoes are tender.
5. To serve: Sprinkle with peanuts; garnish edge of casserole with tomato slices.
Makes 4 to 6 servings.

Baked Spaghetti-and-Cheese Casserole

1 package (8 ounces) thin
spaghetti
1½ cups grated sharp Cheddar
cheese (6 ounces)
1 teaspoon dried oregano leaves
¾ cup chili sauce

2 tablespoons butter or
margarine
¼ teaspoon salt
⅛ teaspoon pepper
1½ cups milk

1. Cook spaghetti, following package-label directions. Drain.
2. Preheat oven to 350° F.
3. In well-greased 2-quart baking dish, place half of spaghetti and half of cheese. Sprinkle with ½ teaspoon oregano; dot with half of chili sauce and 1 tablespoon butter. Add remaining spaghetti and cheese; sprinkle with ½ teaspoon oregano, and dot with remaining butter. Sprinkle with salt and pepper; pour milk over all. Top with remaining chili sauce.

4. Bake, uncovered, 35 to 45 minutes, or until milk is absorbed and cheese is melted.
Makes 6 servings.

California Casserole

¼ cup butter or margarine
1 cup chopped onion
4 cups freshly cooked white rice
2 cups dairy sour cream
1 cup creamed cottage cheese
1 large bay leaf, crumbled
½ teaspoon salt

⅛ teaspoon pepper
3 cans (4-ounce size) green chilies, drained, halved lengthwise, leaving seeds
2 cups grated sharp natural Cheddar cheese

Chopped parsley

1. Preheat oven to 375° F. Lightly grease a 12- by 8- by 2-inch baking dish (2-quart).
2. In hot butter in large skillet, sauté onion until golden—about 5 minutes.
3. Remove from heat; stir in hot rice, sour cream, cottage cheese, bay leaf, salt, and pepper; toss lightly to mix well.
4. Layer half the rice mixture in bottom of baking dish, then half of chilies; sprinkle with half of Cheddar cheese; repeat.
5. Bake, uncovered, 25 minutes, or until bubbly and hot. Sprinkle with chopped parsley.
Makes 8 servings.

Golden Casserole

1 cup raw regular white rice
1 package (10 ounces) frozen chopped spinach
1 can (8 ounces) stewed tomatoes, undrained
1 can (8 ounces) tomato sauce
1 teaspoon grated onion
½ teaspoon dried oregano leaves
⅛ teaspoon garlic powder

1 can (8 ounces) sliced mushrooms, drained
½ cup dry sherry
½ cup fresh bread cubes
1 tablespoon butter or margarine, melted
1 cup grated sharp Cheddar cheese

1. Preheat oven to 350° F.

2. Cook rice and spinach as package labels direct; drain.

3. Combine rice, spinach, tomatoes, tomato sauce, onion, oregano, garlic powder, mushrooms, and sherry; mix well. Turn mixture into a 2-quart casserole.

4. Toss bread cubes with butter; sprinkle top of casserole with bread cubes and cheese.

5. Bake, uncovered, 30 minutes, or until top is golden.

Makes 6 servings.

"Sloppy Joe" Casserole

1 package (8 ounces) shell macaroni	1 can (8 ounces) tomato sauce with cheese
1 envelope (1⁵/₁₆ ounces) Sloppy-Joe-seasoning mix	2 cartons (8-ounce size) creamed cottage cheese
1 pound ground chuck	½ cup grated Cheddar cheese
1 can (6 ounces) tomato paste	

1. Cook macaroni as package label directs; drain.

2. Meanwhile, prepare seasoning mix with ground chuck, tomato paste, tomato sauce, and 1¼ cups water, as package label directs.

3. Preheat oven to 350° F.

4. In 2½-quart casserole, layer one half macaroni, one half cottage cheese, and one half meat sauce; repeat. Top with Cheddar cheese.

5. Bake, uncovered, 40 to 50 minutes, or until bubbling.

Makes 6 servings.

Saturday-Night Bean Bake

2 tablespoons salad oil	1 can (1 pound) tomatoes, undrained
½ cup chopped onion	
½ cup chopped celery	1 teaspoon Italian seasoning
2 cans (1-pound size) pork and beans with tomato sauce	1 pound frankfurters (8)
	1 cup grated Cheddar cheese

1. Preheat oven to 350° F.

2. In hot oil in large skillet, sauté onion and celery until tender—about 5 minutes. Remove from heat. Stir in pork and beans, tomatoes, and Italian seasoning. Turn into a 2-quart casserole. Top with frankfurters.

3. Bake, uncovered, 40 minutes. Sprinkle cheese over top. Bake a few minutes longer, to melt cheese. Serve immediately.

Makes 8 servings.

Spaghetti with White Clam Sauce

4 jars (7½-ounce size) minced clams
⅔ cup olive or salad oil
½ cup butter or margarine
4 large cloves garlic, finely chopped
¼ cup finely chopped parsley
3 teaspoons salt

1 package (8 ounces) spaghetti, cooked and drained
1 package (8 ounces) green noodles, cooked and drained

Grated Parmesan cheese
Lemon wedges

1. Drain clams, reserving 1½ cups liquid and the clams.

2. Slowly heat olive oil and butter in large skillet. Sauté garlic until golden—about 5 minutes.

3. Remove from heat. Stir in the reserved clam liquid, the parsley, and salt; bring to boiling. Reduce heat; simmer, uncovered, 20 minutes.

4. Add clams; simmer 5 minutes, or until heated through.

5. Serve hot over spaghetti tossed with green noodles, with grated cheese and lemon wedges.

Makes 8 servings.

VIII

Speaking of One-Dish Meals

❀ ❀ ❀

The new homemaker quickly learns that cooking has its own special vocabulary. There are literally hundreds of culinary terms; to list and define them all would require another book. However, since we have been talking specifically about one-dish meals—soups, salads, casseroles, and stews—we will explain terms that relate especially to them.

The success of many dishes depends on knowing how to combine the ingredients. Do you know the difference between folding in and cutting in, for example? Or what it means to prepare a roux? Then there are many foreign-language words to recognize—like pot-au-feu and velouté. What are the differences between a terrine and a ramekin? A Dutch oven and a casserole? You will find the answers in the following alphabetized glossary.

Acidify   To add lemon juice or vinegar to a sauce or cooked dish.

Allspice   A spice belonging to the evergreen myrtle family growing in the West Indies. Has a flavor of cinnamon, nutmeg, and cloves. Good with beef stews and gravies.

Anchovy A small Mediterranean fish filleted and preserved in brine or oil, used mainly for salads and for garnish.

Aspic Jelly made from clarified meat stock flavored with herbs and vegetables and set with gelatin.

Au blanc Term signifying a dish that is served with a white or cream sauce.

Au gratin Foods covered with crumbs, butter, and cheese and baked or broiled until top is brown.

Au jus Meats served with natural gravy or meat juices.

Bake To cook by dry heat, usually in the oven. When applied to meats, the process is called roasting.

Baking powder Mixture of cream of tartar and bicarbonate of soda, plus potato starch, corn flour, or rice flour; used as a raising agent.

Barbecue To roast or broil on a rack or revolving spit over or under a source of cooking heat. The food is usually basted with a seasoned sauce.

Basil Aromatic herb used mostly in dishes containing tomato.

Baste To moisten food, usually meat, while it is cooking to add flavor and prevent drying. Melted fat or other liquid may be used.

Batter A mixture of flour, liquid, and other ingredients of a consistency thin enough to pour.

Bay leaf Aromatic leaves from bay, or laurel, tree, used for flavoring stews, soups, and sauces.

Béchamel A basic white sauce.

Beurre Manié Paste made with equal parts of butter and flour used to thicken soups and sauces.

Beurre Noir Literally, "black butter." Butter heated to deep brown color and acidulated with vinegar. When lemon juice is used instead of vinegar, it may be called Beurre Noisette.

Bind Term implying thickening soups and sauces with eggs and cream.

Bisque	Rich cream soup made with fish or shellfish, game, or vegetables.
Blanch	To pour boiling water over food, or to place it in water, bring it to a boil, and drain—to reduce a strong flavor, make firm, or make white.
Blend	To combine two or more ingredients thoroughly.
Boil	To cook in liquid at boiling temperature. Slow boiling will cook just as effectively as rapid boiling.
Bonne Femme	To cook simply, with garnish of vegetables and herbs.
Bordelaise	Indicates dish has been cooked in red wine.
Borsch	Russian and Polish soup flavored with beets and garnished with sour cream. May be clear or contain vegetables.
Bouillabaisse	Soup or stew made with variety of fish and shellfish, a specialty of the French Mediterranean.
Bouillon	Clear soup, broth, or stock made of meat or poultry.
Bouquet garni	A bunch of herbs used to season soups, stews, braised dishes, and sauces. Parsley, thyme, and bay leaves are the foundation; other herbs may be added.
Bourguignon	Indicates dish has been cooked in red wine with bacon, mushrooms, and onions.
Braise	To brown meat or vegetables in a small amount of hot fat, then cover and cook over low heat, sometimes adding a small amount of liquid.
Brochette	Small skewer of wood or metal to hold little pieces of food for grilling or to keep meat or poultry in shape while cooking.
Broth	Liquid in which meat, fish, cereal grains, or vegetables have been cooked; *see* Stock.
Capers	Opened flower buds of a plant grown in southern France and the Mediterranean region. Used in sauces and for garnishing.
Carbonnade	Flemish stew or ragout made with beef and onions and cooked in beer.
Casserole	Cooking utensil with lid, made of earthenware, glazed china, glass, or metal, used for food requiring slow cooking.

Cassoulet	Hot pot of beans made with herbs, pork, mutton, sausage, and sometimes other meats, and originating in France.
Chafing dish	Shallow pan used for cooking food at the table.
Chapon	Slice of French bread rubbed with garlic, sprinkled with vinegar and oil, used in salads.
Chasseur	Literally, "huntsman," indicating a dish of meat or game cooked in white wine with mushrooms.
Chaudfroid	Food prepared hot, then covered with an aspic and served cold.
Chervil	Herb popular in French cookery, usually included in the *fines herbes* in omelets.
Chicory	Curly-leafed salad plant.
Chives	Plant of the onion family, with bright green leaves, which, finely chopped, are used in salads, omelets, soups, and with potatoes and vegetables.
Clarify	As applied to liquid food or fat, it means to render clear or limpid, to suppress the solid parts, or separate solids from liquid.
Cock-a-leekie	A rich broth containing chicken and leeks.
Consommé	Meat or chicken stock that has been enriched, concentrated, and clarified. Served hot or cold.
Cornstarch	Fine starch from maize or Indian corn, used as a thickening agent.
Crab boil (shrimp boil)	A mixture of herbs and spices commercially available, used to enhance crab or shrimp dishes.
Creole	Term applied to highly seasoned dishes with rice, usually with peppers, tomatoes, and okra.
Cress	*See* Watercress.
Croustade	Hollowed cube or round of bread or pastry in which chicken, meat, or game is served.
Croutons	Diced fried or toasted bread used to garnish soups and salads.
Cut in	To distribute solid shortening through dry ingredients by using two knives, a pastry blender, or a fork.
Daube	A method of cooking meat, generally beef, by braising in red wine and stock with herbs.
Dice	To cut in quarter-inch cubes.

Dredge   To coat completely with a dry ingredient such as seasoned flour.

Dumpling   Small balls of dough made from flour and water, simmered in boiling water or stock, served with stews, or cooked in stew with other ingredients.

Dust   To sprinkle lightly with flour or sugar.

Dutch oven   Cast-iron or heavy pot with tight-fitting domed cover.

Émincé   Dish made with leftover roast or braised meat, covered with a sauce.

Émincer   To slice meat, vegetables, or fruit very thinly.

Endive   White, yellowish-tipped compact vegetable used raw in salads or cooked. Imported from France or Belgium. Term *endive* is sometimes applied to chicory.

Escarole   Salad plant with wide dark-green leaves.

Espagnole   A basic brown sauce made with brown meat stock, vegetables, herbs, and wine.

Estouffade   Term applied to dish requiring long slow cooking like a stew. Or a clear brown stock used to dilute sauces or moisten meat dishes.

Fennel   Anise-flavored herb of Italian origin, used in salads, fish dishes, or cooked like celery.

Fines herbes   Mixture of parsley and chervil and other herbs, often used in omelets.

Flamber   To pour brandy (cognac) over food and set it aflame.

Florentine   Indicates spinach is included in ingredients of a recipe.

Fold in   To combine a delicate ingredient such as beaten egg whites with a solid mixture such as a batter, using a gentle under-and-over motion with a wire whisk or rubber spatula.

Fricassee   White stew of veal or chicken.

Garlic   Pungent-flavored bulb of the onion family composed of small divisions called cloves.

Gazpacho	Spanish dish best described as a soup-salad. Served cold, it contains tomatoes, cucumber, onion, and green pepper.
Glaze	A gravy or meat stock reduced by boiling so residue will set when cold. Used to brush over meat dishes.
Goulash	Stew of Hungarian origin made with beef or veal. Highly seasoned, it contains paprika and onion.
Gumbo	A soup thickened with filé or okra pods and usually containing vegetables with meat or seafood.
Hollandaise	Rich sauce made with egg yolks, butter, and lemon juice, served with fish, eggs, and vegetables.
Hot pot	Stew cooked in a deep earthenware dish, usually topped with potatoes.
Hotchpotch	Favorite Scottish soup or stew made with mutton, peas, barley, and diced root vegetables.
Infuse	To extract flavor by steeping.
Irish stew	A white stew of mutton, onion, and potatoes.
Jambalaya	Rice cooked with ham, sausage, chicken, and shrimp or oysters and seasoned with herbs.
Julienne	Method of cutting vegetables and other foods in thin strips. Also, a consommé or clear soup with a julienne garnish.
Kebab	Cubes of meat, such as lamb, marinated and cooked with onions, tomatoes, or other vegetables, usually on a skewer. If not marinated, the cooking method is called *en brochette.*
Kedgeree	Anglo-Indian dish of highly seasoned rice, fish, and egg.
Larding	To insert strips of fat under the skin or into the flesh of meat, fish, or poultry with a skewer or larding needle.
Leek	Vegetable with mild onion flavor often used in soups and stews.

Lentil	The seed of a leguminous plant, it resembles a split pea and is often used for soup.
Liaison	Thickening for sauces, gravies, or stews.
Mace	Dried netlike shell that surrounds nutmeg seed; when ground, used for flavoring vegetables, especially spinach and potatoes.
Marinate	To let food stand in a spicy, often acid mixture to improve flavor and texture.
Marjoram	Aromatic herb used for flavoring lamb, veal, and egg dishes.
Marmite	A French earthenware stock pot or small individual soup cup.
Mirepoix	A mixture of diced root vegetables used as a base for braising meat and for flavoring sauces and stews.
Mornay	A method of preparing fish, eggs, or vegetables in which food is coated with cheese sauce and glazed under a grill or in the oven.
Moussaka	Rumanian, Greek, or Turkish dish of mutton, eggplant, tomatoes, and cheese sauce.
Mousse	A dish, generally served cold, to which stiffly beaten egg whites give special texture.
Mulligatawny	Highly spiced soup flavored with curry.
Navarin	Stew or ragout of lamb containing small glazed onions, carrots, turnips, and potatoes.
Niçoise, salade	Indicates salad dish with many ingredients, often including green beans, tuna, hard-cooked eggs, lettuce, tomatoes, black olives, and anchovies.
Okra	A plant, the young green pods of which are used for making a soup or chicken stew called gumbo. May be served as a vegetable.
Osso buco	Stew made with knuckle or leg of veal cooked with meat on the bone. Tomatoes and white wine are usually in this dish of Italian origin.
Paella	Spanish dish of rice, chicken, shellfish, and vegetables cooked together and flavored with garlic.

Paprika   Hungarian term for pimiento or sweet red pepper. Used in goulash, stews of veal or chicken, and as a garnish.

Parsley   Widely used herb popular for garnishing or flavoring.

Petite marmite   Clear soup of beef marrowbones, chicken giblets, and vegetables, generally served with toast garnish.

Poach   To cook in simmering liquid.

Polenta   Italian name for a preparation of maize or cornmeal.

Pot-au-feu   French dish of beef and vegetables cooked in deep earthenware casserole or marmite.

Provençale   Describing dishes containing tomatoes, oil, and garlic.

Puree   To press food through a fine sieve or food mill, or reduce to pulp in a blender.

Quiche   Custard tart originating in France; originally crisp bacon and onion in rich egg custard.

Ragout   Stew made from regular-size pieces of meat, poultry, or fish.

Ramekin   Individual heatproof dish of china, glass, or earthenware.

Ratatouille   Dish of vegetables cooked together in olive oil; generally eggplant, sweet peppers, onions, tomatoes, and garlic are included.

Ravigote   A sauce, hot or cold, to which tarragon, chervil, chives, white wine, and vinegar have been added. In cold form, it is a mixture of oil and vinegar with chervil, tarragon, parsley, capers, shallots, and other herbs.

Réchauffé   Name given to reheated food.

Reduce   To lessen quantity of liquid by boiling it away over moderately high heat to the desired quantity.

Refresh   To pour cold water over vegetables after they are cooked to preserve color.

Rémoulade   Sauce for cold fish, meat, poultry, or eggs: mayonnaise with anchovies, green onions, capers, gherkins, parsley, chervil, and tarragon.

Render　　　　To heat fat such as suet or salt pork until melted with only the crisp part remaining.

Rosemary　　　An aromatic, spicy herb that goes well with chicken or lamb.

Roux　　　　　A mixture of melted fat and flour used in making sauces and gravies.

Sage　　　　　Herb with a strongly aromatic grayish green leaf, used mostly with onion for stuffings.

Salmis　　　　Ragout made of game, roasted, then stewed in a rich wine sauce.

Sauté　　　　To cook in a small amount of hot fat in a skillet.

Savory　　　Aromatic herb with slightly bitter flavor resembling that of sage, generally used for stuffings and for flavoring soups.

Scald　　　　To heat to just below the boiling point; also to pour boiling water over food or to dip food quickly into boiling water.

Sear　　　　To brown the surface of meat quickly by intense heat.

Shallot　　　Small onion with a delicate flavor like that of garlic.

Shortening　　Term for any fat used for making pastry or cakes.

Simmer　　　To cook below boiling point, generally at about 185° F.

Stew　　　　To cook foods in simmering liquid.

Stock　　　The liquid in which meat, bones, or vegetables have been simmered gently for a long time. Basis for sauces, gravies, and many soups. (Fish stock is made from fish trimmings and parts.)

Tarragon　　　Narrow-leafed herb with mild licorice flavor used in chicken dishes, omelets, and some sauces.

Tartare sauce　Cold sauce for fish: a mayonnaise, chopped gherkins, capers, and herbs combination.

Terrine　　　Earthenware dish, generally oval in shape, with tight lid.

Toss	To tumble ingredients lightly, as with salad greens.
Thyme	Pungent herb of mint family used in bouquet garni and in stuffings.
Unleavened	Usually applied to bread made with flour but no raising agent.
Velouté	Rich white sauce served with meat, poultry, or fish; or a cream soup.
Véronique	Term indicating white grapes have been used in the preparation or in the garnish.
Vichyssoise	Cold cream soup prepared with leeks and potatoes.
Vinaigrette	Spicy dressing for salads and vegetables made with oil, vinegar, and seasonings, and sometimes herbs, finely chopped shallots, gherkins, and capers.
Vol-au-vent	Small pie or puff pastry filled with meat or fish and sauce.
Watercress	Peppery small green plant used in salads, for soups, and in garnishes.
Whip	To beat rapidly with rotary beater, electric mixer, or wire whip to incorporate air and increase volume.
Whisk	Wire beater particularly suitable for beating cream and light mixtures.
Worcestershire sauce	Piquant sauce, highly seasoned, prepared commercially from a base of soy.
Work	As a culinary term, implies mixing or kneading a dough slowly and steadily.
Yogurt	Milk that has been soured with a special culture.

Index